Solving Produc Exercises: Ques Answers

Practice your product design and UX skills. Prepare for your next job interview.

© 2018 Sugar So What Ltd. All rights reserved.

All rights reserved. This book or any portion thereof may not be reproduced or used in any manner whatsoever without the express written permission of the publisher except for the use of brief quotations in a book review.

Artiom Dashinsky
hvoostik@gmail.com
productdesigninterview.com

Editor: Sarah Busby

Table of contents

Introduction — 4
Why I wrote this book — 5
Why should you read this book? — 11

Chapter 1
Introducing the design exercise
The interview process — 13
What is a design exercise? — 15

Chapter 2
How to solve a product design exercise
Answer structure — 24
The framework — 26
Step 1: Understand your goal (Why) — 31
Step 2: Define the audience (Who) — 34
Step 3: Understand the customer's context and needs (When and Where) — 37
Step 4: List ideas (What) — 40
Step 5: Prioritise and choose an idea — 42
Step 6: Solve — 44
Step 7: Measure success (How) — 48
Validating your solution — 50
How much time should you spend on each step? — 50
How to present your solution — 51

Chapter 3
Questions and Answers
3.1. Designing a kiosk interface — 57
3.2. A self-publishing platform for Amazon — 69
3.3. A dashboard for freelancers — 83
3.4. Improving primary health care — 95
3.5. Improving the ATM experience — 110

Chapter 4
How to use a design exercise when interviewing
Chapter 5
Tasks list
    A collated list of all tasks mentioned in the book   130
    Additional tasks   135
Chapter 6
Interviews
    Bobby Ghoshal: how designers should change their mindset   140
    Justin Maxwell: advice for designers who want to become founders   143
    Helen Tran: the skill most designers overlook   145
    Joel Califa: two tips for getting a job   147
    Mia Blume: skills which future design managers should work on   149
Additional Resources
    The interview process   151
    Learning product design and UX   152
    Career advice   153
    Hiring designers   154
    The impact of design   155
Appendix: Design Exercise Canvas

Introduction

We're living in the golden age of design. UX and product designers are doing creative, challenging and well-paid work that has an impact on millions or even billions of people's lives. Increasingly, companies understand the importance of design, designers are getting a seat at the table or become founders of companies themselves.

The best designers don't just have great visual taste, although aesthetics certainly plays a big part. But the most successful designers in our industry today have a deep understanding of how design affects business and its value within the organisation.

Unfortunately, design schools often don't teach all the skills needed to become successful in design roles in tech companies: how design affects business; how to work with engineers; how to present your work to non-designers; how to research and understand customers; how to optimise design to deliver on the business' KPIs (Key Performance Indicators); how to measure a design's performance etc. As an industry we're highly interested in having more highly skilled designers, and I believe we should work on creating better resources to teach design that is beyond aesthetics. We should help our peers and colleagues to understand how they can have impact and grow. This book aims to address this skills gap and encourage sharing of knowledge between designers and businesses to bridge the divide. You'll find tools and techniques that help you to come up with solutions that tackle more than just the visual aspects of design.

I'm convinced that designers who learn how to help companies to solve business problems will help us to build better products and, hopefully, solve the most urgent problems the world is facing today, making it more sustainable, healthy and equal.

Why I wrote this book

Recently, I lead the design of several products at WeWork. WeWork provides businesses and individuals with space, community and services. Its community of more than 175,000 members is spread across more than 200 buildings in 64 cities[1]. Technology is one of the main reasons WeWork grows so rapidly — in 2017 it opened 90 new buildings, entered 31 new cities, growing the community from 80,000 members in 2016 to 175,000 in 2017.

As a part of my role, I was responsible for recruiting design talent in our R&D centre. I interviewed dozens of designers and saw more than 100 portfolios at different levels of seniority. One of the main issues we had with unsuccessful candidates was their failure to understand the designer's role in the context of the business, and beyond aesthetics.

---

[1] "WeWork 2017 Year in Review" https://www.wework.com/blog/posts/wework-2017-year-in-review

Julie Zhuo, VP of Product Design at Facebook, describes the design career path in three steps[2] (Illustration 1):

- Step 1: Craft & Execution — sharpening the basics of design, mastering the tools, getting better at designing clear and visually aesthetic interfaces.
- Step 2: Product Thinking — Julie puts it this way: "Strong product thinking means that you understand what a good outcome is and how to design an experience that would lead to those good outcomes."
- Step 3: Influencing Skills — clear communication, effective collaboration.

Let's look at Step 2: Product Thinking.

Product Design Career Path
(by Julie Zhuo)

Craft & Execution	Product Thinking	Influencing Skills

Illustration 1. Three steps of product design career path by Julie Zhuo

At the top companies, like Facebook, Google and Amazon, designers play a role that is beyond aesthetics, focusing on the product thinking. At these companies, designers make

---

[2] "The Beginning of your Design Career – The Year of the Looking Glass" 13 Feb. 2017, https://medium.com/the-year-of-the-looking-glass/the-beginning-of-your-design-career-549828025494.

sure the company is building the right features for the right people[3]. They are highly aware of the company's business goals, how their work is connected to these goals, who their users are, what their needs are, and how their work success is measured etc.

Design in Tech Report 2017[4] #1 observation is: "Design isn't just about beauty; it's about market relevance and meaningful results." *Future of Design in Startups 2017*[5] survey's #1 conclusion is that designers in technology start-ups need to be involved directly in the business side, understanding company strategy, retention / engagement / conversion metrics, revenue model etc. I believe it's also true for businesses outside of the tech industry.

At the end of the day, businesses exist to generate profits and they will value anyone who will help them to achieve their business goals. Many companies still don't understand that design can deliver these goals. At these companies, designers are expected to work on the first step only — implementing appealing visuals and focusing on how things look. As a result, it's hard for designers to

---

[3] "Why Product Thinking is the next big thing in UX Design - Medium." 5 Jul. 2015, https://medium.com/@jaf_designer/why-product-thinking-is-the-next-big-thing-in-ux-design-ee7de959f3fe

[4] "Design in Tech Report" designintechreport.wordpress.com

[5] "Future of Design in Start-Ups 2017 survey" http://futureof.design

progress in their careers and businesses are not benefiting from the wider value designers could bring.

Here are four reasons for this gap:

"Dribbblisation of Design"

The design community is lucky to have so many great resources like Dribbble, Behance etc. These communities are the biggest and most prominent in the design community. They allow designers to see others' visual work, show their own and get feedback on it. But unfortunately, a saturated market of visual-centric design communities leads to Dribbblisation of Design[6] — an obsession about how things look over how they work. This has created the wrong perception in the minds of both designers and businesses i.e. that Product Design = Dribbble.

Lack of communication between businesses and the design community

The top 1% of companies have figured out how to use designers to achieve business goals. Both businesses and designers at these companies benefit from this, but the knowledge is not shared externally. These companies can afford to compete for the top 1% of talent and educate entry-level designers in-house, so there is no transparency about what skills are required and the product challenges that their designers might face.

---

[6] "The dribbblisation of design - Inside Intercom." https://blog.intercom.com/the-dribbblisation-of-design/.

As a result, entry-level designers don't know what they should aspire to, what skills they should practice and what kind of problems they are expected to be able to solve to be hired by the top 1% of companies.

Different expectations of the role of 'Product Designer'

Often companies use the Product Designer title because the top 1% are doing so and thus they can compete for the same pool of talent.

However, some companies will only expect Product Designers to produce appealing visuals, whereas the top companies will expect them to solve business problems with design. So, in practice, designers can find themselves looking at the same title, or even the same job description, for two different roles.

Lack of educational resources

There is a severe lack of resources that allow designers to practice product thinking. Design schools don't teach the appropriate skills, online courses aren't going deep enough and companies do not share their internal processes or case studies. Thus, during interviews designers are often asked to do something they have never been taught.

As a result:

- Many **companies** don't know how to leverage designers to solve business problems and do not create an appropriate platform for them to grow.
- **Mid-level designers** don't know what they should do to progress in their career, so they move to companies where designers focus on visuals only, and get stuck in a repetitive cycle.
- **Junior designers** don't know what kind of problems they are expected to be able to solve to get hired by the top tech companies, so they keep practicing their visual skills and fill their portfolios with unsolicited visual redesign concepts[7] instead of demonstrating their ability to solve product (and business) problems.

As a first step, in an attempt to minimise these skills gaps, I shared publicly the design exercises we used to interview designers at WeWork. I hoped it would help candidates to better understand what kind of problems they are expected to be able to solve and what skills they should work on. And it did help.

The feedback I received was great. Designers were using these exercises to build their portfolio, prepare for interviews and practice their product design skills. Some of them reached out to me to admit that they didn't even know how to approach these kinds of exercises. That makes sense considering the design school, employers and the design community aren't teaching them to do so.

---

[7] "Why I HATE your FAKE redesign! – Medium." 28 Mar. 2017, https://medium.com/pixelpoint/why-i-hate-your-fake-redesign-177a626d7f95.

This book is my attempt to make sure we, as a design community, provide appropriate resources for designers to increase their awareness of product thinking and how to create value for the businesses they work for. As a result, we'll have better prepared designers and, hopefully, we can move the industry forward.

Why should you read this book?

This book is for anyone who wants to understand the Product Designer role at tech companies, to get a sense of what kind of challenges they are dealing with and to practice solving them. It will especially benefit professionals who are going to interview or be interviewed for Product Design, UX Design and UI/UX Design positions.

More specifically, I'll talk about how hiring processes work at tech companies, and focus on design exercises both from a candidate's and an interviewer's perspective. These exercises are inspired by those used in hiring processes by companies such as Google, Facebook, WeWork and Amazon. Here's how you could benefit:

- **Entry-level designers**
    - Learn and practice skills that are required by the top companies
    - Prepare for your first job interviews
    - Find tasks for building a better portfolio to become more appealing to employers
- **Mid-level and senior designers**

- o Improve product thinking and progress in your career
- o Learn to interview other designers
- o Prepare for the next job interview
- **Anyone making a career shift to product design**
  - o Learn more about the role and practice appropriate skills
  - o Find tasks for your first portfolio
  - o Prepare for your job interview
- **Business leaders**
  - o Learn how to interview your first design hire
  - o Understand the mindset of the most successful designers so as to better define the design role at your organisation
- **Other professionals** (product managers, engineers, data scientists etc.)
  - o Learn to ask the right questions to make better product decisions
  - o Learn to collaborate with designers more efficiently by understanding how they think.

Chapter 1

Introducing the design exercise

The interview process

First, a quick overview of the hiring process at tech companies to understand when design exercises are usually given. The process is different at every company, but here is the general structure that most of them use for hiring product designers:

1. **Phone screening** usually takes between 10-20 minutes and is done by a recruiter or HR person. The main goal of this call is to understand if there is a basic match between you and the hiring company. They'll explain in more depth about the position and ask about your current employment status, past experience and what you, as the candidate, are currently looking for in the role.
2. **An on-site or phone interview** is a deep-dive into your process, tools and dynamics with teams you've worked with. Usually this interview also

includes behavioural questions like "Tell me about a time when you disagreed with a product decision. What happened?" It's also the time when more details about the position are discussed.
3. **Portfolio review** can be combined with the previous step. Sometimes candidates are asked to present their work to the design or product lead or to a broader team of three to five people. You are expected to walk the audience through your projects, explain the objective, how you contributed, what decisions you took and why. The framework presented in this book could help to guide this kind of presentation.
4. *(optional)* **Product/Design critique**. Sometimes, as a part of skills evaluation, a candidate is asked to critique a certain product's design. You may be asked what works, what doesn't, how could it be improved, why the company built this feature etc. The framework presented in this book, together with the guidelines Julio Zhuo suggests in her article *How to do a Product Critique*[8], can be used to prepare for this step.
5. **A design exercise** is a key step in the process that heavily influences hiring decisions. Candidates are asked to solve a product design problem and explain their decisions behind the solution. This book explains exactly how to prepare for the exercise and perfect it.

---

[8] "How to do a Product Critique – The Year of the Looking Glass – Medium." 17 Jun. 2014, https://medium.com/the-year-of-the-looking-glass/how-to-do-a-product-critique-98b657050638.

6. *(optional)* A second **informal interview** is sometimes done to test the company's concerns before issuing an offer i.e. cultural fit, specific aspects of your experience or skills that are lacking.
7. **Offer**.

As you can see, only steps three to five are unique for designers. This book helps to prepare for the design exercise and provides tools that could be used for the design critique and portfolio review.

What is a design exercise?

A design exercise is a design challenge which the interview candidate is asked to solve and present. There are three main types which companies usually use:

- **Live whiteboarding** (15-40 min, on-site) — the candidate is asked to perform the exercise live with the interviewer, explaining their thinking and decisions while solving the task.
- **On-site exercise** (1h, 10-15min presentation and Q&A) — the candidate is given about an hour to solve the problem while being in a comfortable, quiet space equipped with paper and pens. After an hour the candidate will present their solution with wireframes and sketches using a whiteboard.
- **Take-home exercise** (8h-week) — the candidate must deliver a high-fidelity design within a defined deadline (usually four to eight hours). Deliverables will include a presentation and sometimes development-ready source files. Some companies

compensate candidates for the time spent on this exercise.

The type of challenge the candidate is given usually depends on what skills the company requires.

When the company wants to test a candidate's product thinking, it is more likely to be performed on-site with a conceptual task like "design a ATM machine for kids" or "redesign the NYC MetroCard system". When testing visual skills, the company is more likely to ask the candidate to do a take-home exercise focused on UI and visuals, like "design a landing page for a physical product that costs more than $200".

The deliverables will vary as well — from whiteboard wireframes and sketches presented verbally to high-fidelity design delivered via ready-for-development Sketch-files.

You can find a simplified map of exercise types in Illustration 1.1. Keep in mind that the task type could vary depending on the specific role. One of the designers I interviewed during the research for this book, who currently works at Google, said: "Over the past three years I was interviewed by Palantir, Facebook, Apple, Google and Kayak for UX-oriented roles. No process was similar to another. One of these companies asked me to perform a 90-minute design thinking exercise from home. Another required a take-home exercise with a week-long deadline that required low-fidelity deliverables."

Exercises Map

Conceptual task
Tests product thinking, more likely to perform on-site

Live Whiteboarding
15-40min, on-site

Design an ATM machine for kids.

Redesign the NYC MetroCard system.

Improve Spotify.

Onsite exercise
1hr + 10-15min
presentation, on-site

Design an experience for finding an ideal roommate in your city.

LinkedIn decided to build a marketplace for freelancers. Design a flow for hiring a professional.

Take-home exercise
4-8hr net time,
8hr-week deadline

Design a landing page for a physical product that costs more than $200.

Visual-oriented task
Tests visual/UI skills, more likely to perform at home

Illustration 1.1. Simplified map of exercises types for interviewing designers

Types of task

Most of the tasks that candidates are asked to perform are divided into two categories:

1. Build a new product.

- Design a mobile product experience that makes it safe to find the ideal roommate in your city.
- Build a desktop app dashboard for a general practice doctor.
2. Change or improve an existing product.
   - Design a marketplace for freelancers which LinkedIn has decided to build as a part of their product.
   - Pick an underserved audience by Spotify. Suggest how they could improve their offering to this group.

You can look at examples of solutions for each type of these exercises in Chapter 3.

There are two more types of tasks that are rarely asked for, but worth mentioning:
- Conceptual tasks
   - Design an ATM.
   - Design an alarm clock for the blind.
- Business metric-oriented tasks
   - Improve Pinterest's retention.
   - Design a product that creates a new revenue driver for Airbnb.

Why do companies use design exercises?

"It's such a good technique because there's no faking (like showing portfolio work from a big team effort)," writes

Braden Kowitz[9] about design exercises, a former design partner at Google Ventures.

Performing a design exercise tests a designer's skills in an environment as close as possible to the real job, given limited time and resources. In addition, it's a good technique for testing entry-level designers without much prior work or when their previous work is confidential.

Candidates aren't judged solely by the final result. The goal of exercises is to understand how the candidate approaches the problem, what their process is and how they work with the team. In addition to testing product thinking, on-site exercises are a great tool to test candidate's other abilities such as:

- **Communicating** effectively with the team.
- **Thinking critically** and asking good questions.
- **Handling feedback** and constructive criticism.
- **Performing in a high-pressure** environment on a new problem that has a looming deadline.
- **Being the kind of person the team would like to collaborate with** on a day-to-day basis.

As you can see, a design exercise does much more than test the UI-skills of the candidate, and that's why it's so powerful. In most cases, the exercise ends with

---

[9] "How to evaluate a designer with a design exercise - GV Library." 29 Dec. 2011, https://library.gv.com/how-to-interview-a-designer-with-the-perfect-design-exercise-2c99e6646612.

wireframes sketched on a whiteboard so the candidates cannot even fully show their aesthetic skills.

Chapter 2

How to solve a product design exercise

As designers we tend to think visually, so we're tempted to jump right into the final solution and start sketching right away. In both your actual job and in interviews, this approach will most likely lead you to building the wrong product for your audience. The single most important thing you should remember while solving exercises is to **follow a process**. Analysing the problem, asking questions, and evaluating and understanding the audience before doing any visual work is crucial for a successful outcome. In this book, I suggest a framework that I find helpful in solving product design exercises. Feel free to use it as is, or adjust it to fit your needs. Just remember that having a structure could help you in solving and presenting your solutions.

Before we dive in to the framework, here are three tips for solving your challenges.

Make sure you understand the task

It's an obvious one, but skipping it might set you up for a failure. It's extremely important to make sure you and the organisation have the same expectations about:

- Deliverables type (Sketch-files, prototype, presentation etc.)
- Deliveries fidelity level (wireframes or high-fidelity design)
- Presenting — are you required to present your solution?
- Presentation method (phone call, video-conference, email, in person)

Remember that the company would like you to succeed as well, so it is in their interests clarify these things to make sure you have everything needed to demonstrate your skills.

Ask questions and make assumptions

Great designers don't just receive a task and quietly implement it. One of the most important skills of great designers is asking the right questions and making sure they have all the information needed to build the right product for the right audience. Make sure you understand the task and your goal clearly; why this product should exist, who you're building the product for, and what their needs are.

Don't be afraid to ask your interviewer clarifying questions, especially while receiving the task. Understanding your goal clearly will lead to better solutions and make you more confident about them. The interviewer could either answer your question or ask you to decide for yourself and make an assumption. If the latter happens, don't think that you did something wrong, it's a way to test how you operate with limited information.

Even after asking the right questions, you will never have all the information you need to build the perfect product. Eric Ries, author of *Lean Startup,* describes a startup as: "a human institution designed to deliver a new product or service under conditions of extreme uncertainty[10]". Often this uncertainty is true for any new product, even one not built by a startup. In such an environment, you'll have to make **assumptions** and your ability to do this will be tested during interviews.

An assumption is a claim that is backed by little or no data, that is needed to build a successful product or feature. For example, while building a product for restaurant reservations management, you could assume that 20% of all reservations are no shows, which is significant enough to build a solution to help the business avoid losing money.

Be critical about your solutions

Always be aware of the "why" behind your design decisions and be ready to explain them. There are no perfect solutions and your ability to talk about its pros and cons is both important for you and for the interviewer. It will demonstrate your ability to think critically and make

---

[10] "Lessons Learned: What is a startup?." 21 Jun. 2010, http://www.startuplessonslearned.com/2010/06/what-is-startup.html.

you less attached to your ideas and less defensive about them while presenting. In both your actual job and in interviews, this awareness will lead to a better outcome.

For example, when asked to "improve Airbnb" you may suggest building a chatbot. This acts as a personal travel assistant with whom you can chat to book a home and experiences. You assume that such a feature will decrease the friction of using the platform and improve the product's conversion and retention. The downsides you should raise is that building an NLP (Natural Language Processing) product on this scale could be a big engineering effort. In addition, the company will need to hire people to assist in edge cases when technology will fail. Whether you decide to proceed with this solution or not, you should mention both the pros and cons and why you made your final decision.

Answer structure

Solving a design exercise is basically designing a product in an extremely limited time and presenting your thinking process and the result. It means that the process for the exercise is similar to building a real product. The high-level parts of such a process are: understanding what you're building, coming up with a solution and measuring its success.

To go through this process, you can answer six questions — "Five Ws and How" (5W1H):

- **Why** am I building this?

- **Who** am I building it for?
- **When and where** will it be used?
- **What** am I building?
- **How** could I measure it?

Your job during the interview exercise is to demonstrate how you answer these questions and follow a process.

5W1H is a technique used in journalism, research and police investigations for information gathering and problem solving. It is also used in product building: Whitney Hess relies on it during UX research[11], Lewis Lin used it in his CIRCLES Method™[12] to help product managers to prepare for interviews. Since it's such a great technique that has proved itself in other areas of expertise, to make it easier to remember, I based my framework on it, which we'll talk about soon.

Questions are partially your answers

The task itself will already include some inputs that will help you to answer some of the 5W1H (but normally won't include the H). Here are some variations of the same task with different W inputs given:

- Design a product to improve freelancers' *(who)* workflow.

---

[11] "The Five W's of UX - 52 Weeks of UX." 23 Jul. 2010, http://52weeksofux.com/post/890288783/the-five-ws-of-ux.

[12] "Decode and Conquer" https://www.amazon.com/Decode-Conquer-Answers-Management-Interviews/dp/0615930417.

- Design a web app dashboard *(what)* to improve freelancers' workflow *(who)*.
- The global workforce is moving towards a higher percentage of freelancers and contractors. Freelancers don't have a single product to manage their client workflow and every hour they spend on managing their business means investing less time in what they love to do and earning less money *(why)*. Design a web app dashboard *(what)* to help freelancers *(who)* manage, monitor, and plan their client work.

As you can see, the more inputs there are, the more guidance we have towards the final solution and the more time we have to spend producing it.

In the next section we'll learn to answer each of 5W1H questions.

The framework

The framework may feel like a lot of work at first, but after practicing this technique you'll see that most of the steps take just a couple of minutes and the transition between them feels natural. I also prepared a framework canvas that will guide you through it and help you to remember the framework. You can print it on an A4 sheet of paper and practice solving exercises listed at the end of this book. Read more about the canvas in the Appendix. I also prepared a Cheat Sheet (Illustration 2.1) for the framework which you can glance at to remind yourself of the next step and what questions to ask.

While building a real product, most of the framework steps are usually defined in collaboration with other team members — product managers, data analysts etc. So, don't panic if you feel stuck during any of these steps, or if you don't feel you got it perfectly. However, the single step you must perfect is Step 6, where you have to demonstrate your UI/UX skills. These are the core skills a designer at any level of seniority is expected to have and, unlike other steps, there is a chance you're the only person in the company who will be able to solve it.

Finally, before we dive into the framework — don't follow it blindly. Like any framework, it can't perfectly fit every task, so use your judgement as to when to apply it. However, I'm confident that you'll find some tools that will be very helpful in solving any product design exercise.

Framework Cheat Sheet

① **Why**
Understand your goal

- Why is this product or feature important?
- What problem are we trying to solve?
- What impact does it have on the world?
- How does this product benefit customers?
- What business opportunities does it create?

  For existing products, in addition to the above:
- How does it extend the company's mission?

② **Who**
Define the audience

- What are the categories of people who have significantly different motivations for using this product? Pick one.
  - What are the different groups inside this audience that have different needs?

    Age, gender, location, occupation, mobility etc.

(3) When and Where
Understand customer's context and needs

List the context and conditions (When and Where)

> Where are they physically?
> Is there a trigger event causing this need?
> How much time do they have?
> Are they on a specific digital app or platform?
> What emotions do they experience?

List customers' needs

> What is the customer's high-level motivation for solving the problem?
> How could they achieve that?

(4) What
List ideas (A, B, C...)

> What could the company build to fulfill the customer's needs?
>> Type of product: physical/digital
>> Smart watch, smartphone, tablet, desktop, laptop, TV, VR-headset etc.
>> Type of interface — graphic, audio/voice, VR, AR etc.

(5) Prioritise and choose an idea

> Place ideas on an Impact/Effort matrix:

Impact vs. Effort diagram

Implementation effort vs.
Reach, value for customer, potential revenue

(6) Solve

> Storyboarding

Map out the customer's journey to get a picture of what interactions your product needs to support.

> Defining tasks

Make a list of tasks the customer needs to complete to use your product successfully.

> Speedy sketching

Sketch four possible interfaces for the product you're trying to design. Spend one minute per sketch.

7 **How**
Measure success

> How would we know that the solution was successful?
>
> Task success rate, task completion time, engagement, retention, revenue, conversion, user acquisition, net promoter score (NPS).

Illustration 2.1. Cheat sheet for the framework steps

Step 1: Understand your goal (Why)

I like how Erika Hall defines design "it's the gap between what currently exists and what you're aiming for[13]". A great way to start your solution and presentation is to define what it is that you're aiming for and how it helps the business.

Building a new product

Whether you're doing a live whiteboard exercise or preparing a keynote that will be sent over email, a great way to start your presentation is answering the questions:
- Why is this product or feature important?
- What problem are we trying to solve?
- What impact does it have on the world?
- How does this product benefit customers?
- What business opportunity does it create?

---

[13] "Erika Hall: Asking "why?" on Vimeo." 26 Oct. 2015, https://vimeo.com/143660646.

One of the exercises we used at WeWork was a redesign of the NYC MetroCard experience. Here is a great way to start the presentation of such a task:

"The NYC MetroCard system has remained unchanged for decades. Its redesign is an opportunity to improve the transportation infrastructure in one of the biggest cities in the western world, which could decrease pollution, provide access to better education and employment opportunities, improve the health of millions of citizens and potentially save the economy an enormous amount of money".

If you feel that you have more time, you could describe the status quo i.e. what's the current situation and what problems seem to be out there:

"The NYC MetroCard system has remained unchanged for decades. The high cost of the MetroCard machine infrastructure, and the ease of gaming the system by swiping your card for others, has cost the city millions of dollars. New Yorkers who have lost time waiting in line to buy a MetroCard, had to touch a dirty machine to do it, and feared losing their easily misplaced MetroCard, may find other types of transportation more appealing.

The MetroCard redesign is an opportunity to improve transportation in one of the biggest megalopolis where better public transportation could decrease pollution, provide access to better education and employment opportunities, improve the health of millions of citizens and potentially save the economy an enormous amount of money".

Improving an existing product

When being asked to improve an existing product, you can use a similar tactic. **Think about the vision, the "why" of the company and how your improvement supports it.** Then translate this vision to a business opportunity it creates.

Let's say the task is as follows: "LinkedIn decided to build a marketplace for freelancers. Design a flow for finding a professional using such a marketplace." A great way to start your presentation is:

The LinkedIn mission is to connect the world's professionals and to make them more productive and successful. The world's workforce is moving towards becoming more independent. We'll see more and more professionals becoming freelancers and their top priority is finding new clients.

LinkedIn already has a wide range of audiences from both sides of this marketplace — freelancers and businesses interested in their services. Building this marketplace is a great extension of the company's mission that manages to leverage its existing audience, increase its value to customers and provide the company with another revenue stream.

Step 2: Define the audience (Who)

After defining your vision you should **understand who are you building a product for**.

This is how Paul Graham, founder of Ycombinator, describes the high-level reason startups fail and, by extension, the reason a product fails: "In a sense there's just one mistake that kills startups: not making something users want. If you make something users want, you'll probably be fine, whatever else you do or don't do. And if you don't make something users want, then you're dead, whatever else you do or don't do.[14]" By not truly understanding your target audience, you're risking building something users don't want. That's why this step is crucial.

Choose the audience

To understand the various high-level types of audience for the product, ask yourself — **what are the categories of people who have significantly different motivations for using this product**? For example, for Spotify it would be listeners, artists and business owners. For a marketplace of doctors it would be doctors and patients.

Considering the limited time given for the exercise, you should focus on a single high-level audience from whose

---

[14] "The 18 Mistakes That Kill Startups - Paul Graham." http://paulgraham.com/startupmistakes.html.

perspective you would like to show your solution. Pick one of the two biggest audiences, so you will have enough scope for coming up with ideas of how to serve them. So, for Spotify, you would probably choose listeners or artists. For a marketplace of doctors, you would preferably go with patients.

One thing you should keep in mind: sometimes a product's audience or user and the customer are not the same. This is usually the case for B2B2C solutions. For example, if you're building an appointment-scheduling system for clinics, your users will be patients and clinic personnel (doctors, nurses, receptionists). However, the customer to whom this product will be sold is clinics. Most probably it won't change the solution, but it's something worth remembering and mentioning during the presentation.

Describe the audience

Once we choose the high-level audience, we want to better understand the people we're building a product for. To do that, ask yourself 'what characterises our audience?' Here are some of the classifications you could use:

- Age (think how differently Snapchat would be designed if their target audience was adults aged above 50)
- Gender (81% of Pinterest users are women. It would be hard to ignore this while building new features)
- Location (Spotify is more likely to be streamed to Apple TV when used at home and more likely to be listened to with headphones at work)

- Occupation (real estate agents spend less time in front of their computer than software engineers, but more time on their cell phones)
- Mobility (transportation type, travel habits, commuter preferences — Amazon's Audible mobile app has a car mode with an adjusted interface, since it's commonly used during car commuting)

When your task is to come up with a new product/feature, it is useful to list different groups inside of this audience that you think have different needs. It will help you to find dedicated solutions for specific groups of users when you tackle the next steps.

Let's say your task is "improve the Spotify mobile experience". The first step would be listing high-level audiences: listeners, artists, business owners. You decide to go with listeners. Spotify has already made headway with this differentiation of listeners, providing dedicated features for runners, club music lovers, podcast listeners etc. You could develop ideas for new interesting features by listing different groups, for example, by age:

- Children (a feature that allows parents or even teachers to use Spotify for audio lessons for children)
- Millennials (spend a lot of time listening to music and being with friends[15]. I assume they also do these things together.You could suggest building a shared Play Queue, so a group of friends could add songs to play on Spotify on the background)

---

[15] "What Do Millennials Like To Do With Their Free Time?" https://www.marketingcharts.com/television-29750

- Baby boomers (they are more likely to live in the suburbs and commute by car into the city. You could suggest building a podcast or audiobook experience tailored for a car commute).

Step 3: Understand the customer's context and needs (When and Where)

Once you have defined your audience, the next step is to understand **when and where they experience this problem, and how you can solve it**. This information will help us to understand what kind of product and features we should build in the next steps.

List the context and conditions (When & Where)

First, think about the environment in which the audience defined in Step 2 is having the problems described in Step 1. Here are some questions to help you explore the context of your users:
- Where are they physically?
- Is there a trigger event causing this need?
- How much time do they have?
- Are they on a specific digital app or platform?
- What emotions do they experience?

Let's say the task is "redesign Waze to support bike rides". This feature is going to be used during a commute. A commuter on a bike wants to look at their smartphone as little as possible, and often in difficult conditions such as at night or during bad weather. In the next steps, we'll take these circumstances into consideration while coming up with a solution. It might mean allowing hands-free navigation or a dark interface at night etc.

List the audience's needs

Now we want to understand the needs that our product needs to fulfill. To do that we should ask "what is the customer's high-level motivation for solving the problem we're tackling?" For example, when undertaking a task "design a product for managing a freelance business", the customer's high-level motivation would be "being in control of their business".

Sometimes this list will be enough to give you ideas for products that could be built to meet these needs. In most cases, you'll need to dig a little deeper. Look at the high-level motivation we defined and ask yourself **"how could they achieve that?"**

Using the freelancers example, in order to be in control of their business, they need to know:
   a. How their business is doing financially
   b. How they should plan their work
   c. What they can do to move their business forward.

The 'user stories' technique

This technique is relatively time-consuming, so I'd recommend to use it during take-home exercises, or while practicing. It helpsto explore the user's context and needs and the connection between them. You might already be familiar with this technique, since it's used in Agile methods of software development. To create user stories, use natural language to fill out this template using your knowledge of the audience:

As a <role>, I want <goal/desire> so that <benefit>

The *goal/desire* is what the user wants to achieve with your product. The *benefit* is the reason they want to achieve this goal — the real motivation for performing it. So, going back to the Waze task, some example user stories could be:

- *As a bike commuter, I want to navigate without distracting myself from the road, so that I can commute safely.*
- *As a bike commuter, I want to use a touch interface as little as possible when it's raining or when I use gloves, so I can get to my destination faster and safer.*
- *As a bike user, I want to know if it's safe to leave my bike outside in my chosen destination, so that I can avoid it being stolen.*
- *As a bike user, I want to know what to do in case of a flat tyre, so I can get to my destination on time.*

Identifying the problems

Another technique for generating ideas is mapping out the current customer journey and identifying any problems that can be transformed into opportunities later on. For example, if you map out how people are using ATM machines you can easily come up with a list of suboptimal experiences: possible queue, need to remember the PIN code and your card, touching a dirty machine, being exposed to card fraud etc. All of these could give you ideas for a product or a feature during the next steps.

Step 4: List ideas (What)

Now is the time to explore **what the company could build to fulfill the customer's needs** defined in the previous step. List three or four possible products. Use these properties to help generate different ideas:

- Type of product — should it be a digital or a physical product? Or maybe your solution is making a physical product "smart" by adding technology. Even though you're not an industrial designer, being able to describe such a solution that is not your area of expertise will definitely give you bonus points.
- Platform — smartwatch, smartphone, tablet, desktop, laptop, TV, VR-headset etc.
- Type of interface — graphic, audio/voice, VR, AR etc.

Your first impression of how Waze could serve bike riders might be adding another mode to their mobile app. But exploring different properties can help you to think about a wider spectrum of possible products that could achieve that — digital or physical, mobile app or smartwatch app, graphic interface or voice interface and more. A list of ideas for the Waze exercise could be presented like that:

Here are several possible solutions, assuming Waze has the biking routes data:
- ***Build a physical product*** *that is installed on the bike steering wheel and indicates to the rider the next turn and how far away it is. The product integrates with the user's smartphone via Bluetooth and displays driving instructions via a set of LED-indicators on the device.*
- ***Adjust the current smartphone app*** *design to include a biking navigation option. The user would receive their riding instructions via speaker or headphones while the smartphone is in their pocket, or visually while the smartphone is mounted on the steering wheel or taken out of the pocket.*
- ***Build a smartwatch app*** *that would take advantage of haptic technology and communicate with the user via tactile feedback over their wrist.*

If you feel a little bit stuck, you can use this template to kick off the process:

Build X for <Who / Step 2>, that <When and Where / Step 3> to <Why / Step 1>.

For example: Build a VR app for people with post-traumatic stress disorder, who avoid getting treatment because of its cost, to help them live better lives and create a new source of income for our business.

Step 5: Prioritise and choose an idea

Once you have explored what could be built to solve the problem, it's time to **choose the idea you believe is optimal**. But how do you know which one to choose?

From the examples above, you can see that there is no single perfect solution. There will always be upsides and downsides for each solution. During this step, we want to evaluate all of them. Here are four considerations that will help you to weigh up each idea:

- Reach — how many customers this product could potentially reach.
- Value for customer — how satisfying this solution is for the customers.
- Potential revenue — how well this solution meets the business goals of the company.
- Implementation effort — how hard it would be for the company to build.

To make it a little bit easier, use an effort / impact matrix. Place each solution on a graph with two axes: impact (combination of reach, value, revenue) and effort:

Impact / Effort Matrix

Great	Good
OK	Bad

Impact (vertical axis), *Effort* (horizontal axis)

Illustration 2.2. Impact / Effort Matrix for prioritizing ideas

In real life, you want to be in the "great" area, which represents quick wins. For the design exercise though, make sure that ideas placed in this area are sophisticated enough to demonstrate your design talent. If it's not, aim to place it in the "good" area.

While presenting, explain why you believe the impact and effort for each solution is high/low, especially for the idea you choose to move forward with. For example, a smartwatch app could provide the best experience, but there is a good chance that only a small number of customers own a smartwatch. So, although it may succeed in solving the user need, the minimal reach would translate to a low impact. Or maybe a physical product seems like the best solution, but the company has never built a physical product before, which means it'll need to work with an external agency or hire industrial designers. In this case, the huge effort required might be not worth it.

Step 6: Solve

It might feel like you've come a long way without starting work on the actual solution. However, you will see that following a process will make it easier to come up with the final product, leading to a better solution and one you can feel confident about.

As I mentioned before, this is the one step in which you can't fail. Doing it poorly will significantly decrease your chances of getting hired. In this step, you'll have to demonstrate your UI/UX skills.

If you're working on an on-site exercise, the deliverables of this step are:
- Wireframe flows
- User journeys
- A list of ideas
- Sketches of any kind.

For take-home exercise, the final deliverables would be high-fidelity designs, but all the techniques described in this step could be used to create a foundation for the high-fidelity solution.

Considering the limited time, you should focus on one or two major flows in your solution. For example, if you redesign a metro card system, a good strategy would be to focus on two main flows — for an occasional commuter (an-out-of-town visitor) and a recurring customer (every day work commuter).

Here are three techniques – storyboarding, defining tasks and speedy sketching – that will help you kick off the design of the product:

Storyboarding

In this technique, you should **map out the customer's journey to get a picture of what interactions your product needs to support**. Exploring these interactions will start giving you some ideas for the interface.

To create a storyboard, map out the steps your customer goes through to successfully use your product.. Sketch each of the steps in the form of a story, considering the customer's context. See an example of a storyboard for the experience of ordering an Uber in Illustration 2.3.

Consider the step before the customer interacts with your product and the step after to see if your product could bring value to these steps as well. For example, in the Waze task, after the bike commuter arrives at their destination, their interaction with the app would normally end. But now the customer needs to decide if it's safe to lock up their bike outside. Waze could collect data about bike theft in different neighborhoods and suggest if it's safe to leave it outside.

Uber Ordering Storyboard

Request a car	Wait while Uber find a car	Check ETA for arriving
Leave the app	Driver notifies they have arrived	Looking for the car outside
Driver and customer identify each other	Commute	Leave

Illustration 2.3. Storyboard example of an experience of requesting an Uber

Defining tasks

This is probably the quickest and most efficient technique to kick off designing your interface. It is similar to storyboarding, but where storyboarding is linear and covers only one main flow, defining tasks allows you to think about different flows.

Make a list of tasks the customer needs to be able to complete to use your product successfully. For example, some of the tasks in the Waze bike commuters example would be:

- *Enter your destination*
- *Change your destination*
- *Cancel your trip*
- *Understand your next action to stay on the right path*
- *Check if you're on the right path*
- *Understand when you've reached your destination*

As you can see, it's a quick 'n' dirty technique to describe a product flow and is recommended for whiteboarding sessions, considering the limited time.

Speedy sketching

If you're doing a take-home exercise and you have enough time, or you're feeling stuck, try this. Fold a sheet of paper in four sections. Take one minute or less to sketch a possible interface for the product you're trying to design — one solution per section. The sketches shouldn't be perfect, but as unique as possible. If you feel that you have more ideas, turn over the sheet and keep sketching.

The goal of this technique is to challenge your mind to come up with more than just the first and most obvious solution and to generate a range of ideas that you can pick from or combine.

Step 7: Measure success (How)

Coming up with a solution doesn't help much if you don't know to measure its success. Now is the time to close the loop and define how you can validate the solution. To do that ask yourself a question. **How would we know that the solution was successful?**

Normally, measuring success includes defining metrics (KPIs) we want to measure and the number that would be considered a success. For the design exercise, you only need to suggest the former.

Here are some example metrics you could use to measure the success of your design:

- Task success rate — the percentage of correctly completed tasks by users.
- Task completion time — the time it takes for the user to complete the task.
- Engagement — how often users interact with the product in a desirable way.
- Retention — how often a desirable action is taken by users.
- Revenue — in what way does the product make money and how much does it make?

- Conversion — the percentage of users who take a desired action.
- User acquisition — persuading the customer to purchase a company's goods or services.
- Net promoter score (NPS) — customer satisfaction measured through their willingness to recommend the company's products to others.

Let's say your task is "design an app dashboard for family doctors", with a goal of increasing the number of patients a doctor serves per day. This is how you could present your suggestion for measuring product success:

The final thing I would do before the launch is to make sure we define KPIs that will indicate the success of this solution and the numbers which would be considered a success. If this solution is successful we'll see:
- *A decrease in the time spent by the doctor per patient*
- *Either retained or improved patient NPS (to ensure the time decrease doesn't impinge on service quality)*

With a real product, the final call on these aspects will be made by a product manager or a data analyst. But, as a product designer, you should be aware of the importance of these factors to your design and demonstrate this to the interviewer. Even if you're not sure of the specific KPIs you should measure, you could say:

As a final step, before shipping this product, I'd work with the product manager to understand what KPIs we should measure and what would be considered a success.

***

Validating your solution

If you have time, you can earn bonus points for suggesting an MVP or an experiment you could run to validate the solution. In the real world, the company probably wouldn't invest several months of development before validating that this product has good potential. However, being aware of this on the ideation step is a good way to build a better product and showing your thoroughness to the interviewer will position you as a more thoughtful designer.

How much time should you spend on each step?

Each step might look like a lot of work, but after some practice you'll see that most of them take just several minutes. Here is how I'd suggest distributing your time while working on a one-hour on-site exercise:

- Step 1: Understand your goal (Why) — 3min
- Step 2: Define the audience (Who) — 5min
- Step 3: Understand customer's context (When/Where) and needs— 5min
- Step 4: List ideas (What) — 5min
- Step 5: Prioritize and choose an idea — 3min
- Step 6: Solve — 30min
- Step 7: Measure — 3min
- Review and prepare for the presentation — 5min

Total: 59min

Depending on the task, you'll have the answers to some steps already provided. If this is the case, use this time for the solution step, which should take at least 50% of the overall time.

How to present your solution

Whiteboarding and on-site exercises

Since the goal of these exercises is to evaluate a designer's thinking, the presentation should include all of the thinking that led to the solution. This means that your presentation should include all of the steps described in the framework above.

While doing a whiteboarding session, sometimes it might be difficult to think and solve at the same time. If that's the case and you feel stuck on one step, your approach should be to *explain the step*. For example, if you're struggling to work out the audience's context you could say out loud: "I'm trying to think about the context of our users — when and where our audience might be dealing with this problem, how do they feel, how much time do they have".

There are three things that could happen:
- Saying it out loud will help you to think about the answer to these questions.
- The interviewer will help you with the answer. If it happens, don't get nervous. It doesn't

automatically decrease your chances of getting hired.
- None of the above — in this case consider moving on to the next step.

If you're afraid of forgetting the steps during the whiteboarding session, you could start your presentation by listing the steps you're going to take the interviewer through, and writing them on the whiteboard, which will provide you with a prompt:

"To make sure we come up with a successful product, first I'll map out the steps of my thinking process. We need to understand why we are building this and what problem we are trying to solve [writes "Why"], who are we building it for [writes "Who"], what their context and needs are [writes "When/Where?"]. Then I'll think about what we can build to fulfill these needs [writes "What"]. After coming up with a solution [writes "Solve"] I'll define how we would measure the solution's success [writes "How"].

Take-home exercises

Considering you'll be asked to send the deliverables via email, I strongly recommend preparing a clickable prototype and not a static image, along with a short presentation explaining your decisions behind the final solution.

The flow of such a presentation could include:
- The task itself
- Problems/vision definition (Why)
- Target audience (Who)

- Context and needs (When & Where)
- The idea you chose to design (use the Message Map technique by Carmine Gallo[16] to come up with a one or two sentence definition of your idea).
- Link to a prototype
- Visual solutions you want to emphasise which can't be explained in the prototype: - grid, design/colours system, accessibility, specific features functionality etc.
- Metrics to measure success (How)

Additional presentation tips

Here are several things to consider in your presentation that could give you extra points:
- Scope — in the presentation of your take-home exercise, explain what your solution addresses and what it does not. Mention what you would do if you have more time. It would create a clear picture of the constrains you operated in.
- Mention blindspots — in case your solution relies heavily on assumptions, suggest a way to conduct research or extract the data to validate it.
- Dosome quick 'n' dirty research — while having enough time during a take-home exercise, run a quick user research for your biggest assumption using a survey or *usertesting.com* and present your results.
- Competitive analysis — your design's goal is to help the business to achieve its goals. These are

---

[16] "Message Map: How To Pitch Anything In 15 Seconds | Forbes - YouTube." 19 Jul. 2012, https://www.youtube.com/watch?v=phyU2BThK4Q.

sometimes set because of the competitors. That means that your design or product solutions will be affected by the products of direct and indirect competitors. If that's the case, position your solution in this context. To quickly analyse the competition , ask yourself these two questions:
- Do they have a similar product or feature? If not, your solution could be a differentiator and help the business to enter or create a new market.
- How good is their solution? Your solution has the potential to outperform your competitors or to minimise the gap between the two.
- Ecosystem — when interviewing with big tech (Amazon, Apple, Microsoft, Facebook and Google) keep in mind that they have a business in many verticals. When coming up with a solution, suggest a way it could be integrated with other parts of the company's ecosystem. For example: while designing a book publishing flow for iBooks, you could suggest authors purchase writing apps from the App Store to help them produce a better result. Or even consider giving away the apps for free if we see evidence that it will help them to publish a successful book.

Chapter 3
Questions and Answers

In this chapter, I'd like to give you a sense of how the design exercises I've discussed in the book could be solved using the framework outlined in Chapter 2.

Below are five individual tasks which I have worked through. Most of them are relevant for whiteboarding or on-site interviews, and all of them can be used as a take-home challenge, if you are given enough time.

I decided not to include high-fidelity implementation for take-home exercises, since there are already many resources that could teach you to do that. Instead, I have focused on the solution flow and product thinking described in the book.

You can also find an example of how the framework canvas (see Appendix) can be used for solving exercises. You can find it in the "Improving primary health care" exercises (3.4).

In case you want to practice solving these exercises first and then check the suggested solutions, you can find a list of them below. Obviously, there is no single right solution for these exercises, so if your solutions are different from those suggested here (which will most probably happen), don't feel that your solution is wrong.

Tasks list:

3.1. Design a kiosk for liquid soap and shampoo refill.

3.2. 81% of Americans want to write a book[17]. In fact, 31% of all e-book sales in the Kindle store are of self-published e-books. Design a product for self-publishing a book on Amazon, decreasing the entry barrier to self-publishing.

3.3. Design a business management dashboard for a freelancer.

3.4. Primary care is associated with enhanced access to healthcare services, better health outcomes and fewer people going to hospital. It also correlates with a more equitable distribution of healthcare within a population. Today, the US healthcare system faces a significant shortage and inequitable distribution in the primary care workforce. Design a digital product to make primary care more accessible.

3.5. Improve the ATM experience.

---

[17] "Think You Have a Book in You? Think Again" — New York Times
http://www.nytimes.com/2002/09/28/opinion/think-you-have-a-book-in-you-think-again.html

3.1. Designing a kiosk interface

Task: Design a kiosk for liquid soap and shampoo refill.

This is a challenge combining both physical and digital experiences which lends itself to an on-site exercise. Here is an example of an ideal interviewer-interviewee interaction to begin this challenge:

Interviewer: We want you to design a kiosk for liquid soap and shampoo refill.

Candidate: Great, where is this product going to be placed? Companies providing living spaces (hotels, hostels, co-living spaces) or retailers (supermarkets, convenience stores, beauty salons, pharmacies) could be interested in this product.

Interviewer: Let's focus on the retail market, specifically supermarkets and convenience stores.

Candidate: OK, how about the physical part of the kiosk, can I modify it?

Interviewer: The kiosk has a touch-screen, two sinks — one for shampoo and one for soap - and a credit card reader. You can't modify the hardware.

Candidate: Great, is there just one type of each product or more?

Interviewer: There are three variants for each product.

Step 1: Understand your goal (Why)

I feel like this product has two main value propositions for the end customer:
- It's sustainable — refilling eliminates unnecessary and wasteful plastic packaging, lessening its impact on the environment. In addition, shampoo and soap are basic products that everyone needs, so our product doesn't promote unnecessary consumption.
- It provides great value — I assume that soap and shampoo are high-margin products that are easy and cheap to produce. Therefore I believe there is an opportunity to create a product that undercuts competitors' price points, considering the easier distribution and lack of packaging, while maintaining or increasing quality.

These two aspects, in addition to a unique delivery system, could create a retail revolution in how products of this type are sold and the concept could be expanded to include products like dishwashing liquid, hair conditioner, fabric softener etc.

For partner stores, this could potentially create a retention driver, that could keep our customers loyal.

Step 2: Define the audience (Who)

Shampoo and soap, as basic commodities, have a huge potential market. They're bought by all adults around the world. Considering the two aspects of eco-friendliness and great value, here are the specific audiences that our product would appeal to:

- **The eco-conscious**. Our product is potentially the most sustainable solution on the market, so I believe it could attract customers who appreciate eco-friendly products.
- **Millennials** are conscious both about environment and their consumption habits and also the most open to changing their habits.
- **Urban citizens**. Considering the kiosks need to be placed in high-traffic environments, I assume they will be placed mostly in cities.
- **Low-income citizens**. Assuming our product will have a lower price than competitors, it would appeal to people who are looking for the best value.

Step 3: Understand the customer's context and needs (When and Where)

Now let's see in what conditions our product will be used. It will be placed inside supermarkets and convenience stores which means:

- A possible queue
- It will be indoors
- There will be decent lighting conditions
- Customer's hands might be busy with shopping bags

When I think about the motivation for buying shampoo or soap, it is very unsophisticated. A desire to maintain a basic level of hygiene is basic and hard-wired into the customer lifestyle. They don't need to be convinced of its merit. Customers can already fulfill that need by buying shampoo or soap somewhere else. So, from a product perspective, our work is to make sure the kiosk provides a seamless customer experience for fulfilling this need.

Before we start exploring the solution, I think there are two extra reasons why the kiosk interface has to be clear and efficient:
- I will assume a queue frightens away customers and decreases sales. A more efficient interface that requires less time to operate would mean fewer queues and more sales.
- The kiosk may often be operated with one hand, since customers would be holding their shopping bags and trying to find the bottles they brought for shampoo and soap refills.

Step 4: List ideas (What) + Step 5: Prioritize and choose an idea

We already know what product we're building, so steps 4 and 5 are unnecessary.

Step 6: Solve

Let's sketch a quick storyboard of a customer's interactions with the kiosk (Illustration 3.1):
- Wait in a queue (if there is one)
- Approach the kiosk
- Pick a product, a flavour, and an amount
- Pay
- Place a bottle underneath
- Wait while it is filled
- Collect the bottle and leave.

1. Approach the kiosk

2. Pick a product, a flavour, and an amount

3. Pay

4. Place a bottle

5. Wait for it being filled

6. Collect the bottle

Illustration 3.1. Storyboard for user journey of refilling soap or shampoo using the kiosk

Now let's visualize the physical part of the kiosk (illustration 3.2). We said that it has:
- A screen
- Two sinks
- A card reader

I'd place the physical sinks under where the products are shown on the screen. That would create a visual connection and educate the customer about where the soap and shampoo sinks are. The card reader could be placed on the right edge of the kiosk, as most people are right-handed.

3.2

Illustration 3.2. Physical representation of the kiosk.

To start mapping out the interface, I'll take a use-case of a customer purchasing 200ml of soap and 400ml of shampoo.

The default screen's goal is mostly promotional (illustration 3.3). It is used as a "banner" to grab the attention of people walking past and to communicate the service's value. We can use a marketing headline like "Zero Plastic Skin & Hair Care" with a more specific description "Shampoo & Soap Refill". At the bottom we'll have an instruction for how to start operating the kiosk: "Click anywhere to start".

```
┌─────────────────────┐    ┌─────────────────────┐
│                     │    │    Bottle Ruler ›  Help › │
│                     │    │                     │
│  Zero Plastic Skin  │    │   Soap    Shampoo   │
│    & Hair Care.     │    │    ◯       ◯       │
│                     │    │    ≡       ≡       │
│  Shampoo & Soap Refill │ │   0ml ⊕   0ml ⊕    │
│                     │    │  $0.76/100ml  $0.93/100ml │
│                     │    │                     │
│ CLICK ANYWHERE TO START │ │                 │
└─────────────────────┘    └─────────────────────┘
         3.3                        3.4
```

Illustration 3.3. Kiosk's default screen.
Illustration 3.4. Product choice screen.

Once the customer touches the screen, they would land on the product selection screen with its description and price (illustration 3.4). Once the quantity of the product is selected, more relevant details, like flavour and total price would appear (illustration 3.5). For each product we'd have:

- Product name
- An icon in a colour representing the selected flavour
- Flavour selection controller opening a modal window (illustration 3.6)
- Controller adjusting the amount of product with 100ml steps. Milliliters don't say much to most people, so to help them relate the measure to something more tangible, we can display an approximate amount of uses this would provide (e.g. 200ml of soap = 120 uses)

- Price per unit
- Total price for the selected amount.

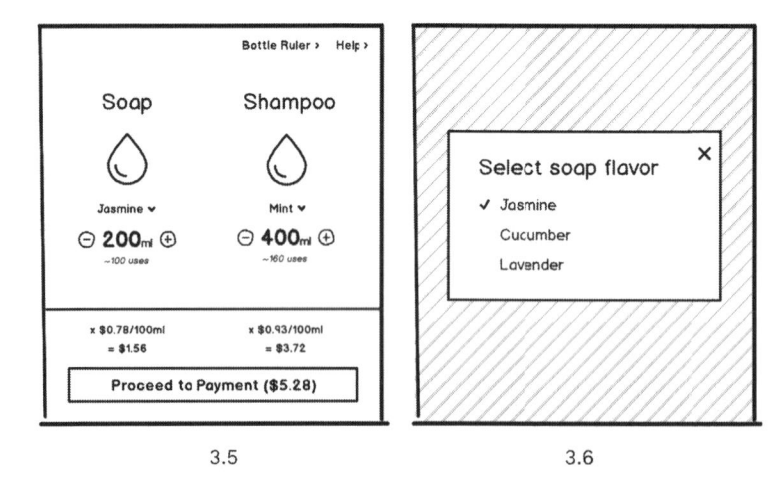

3.5

3.6

Illustration 3.5: Products added by customer and checkout area.
Illustration 3.6: Flavour pick modal window.

The "Proceed to payment ($5.28)" button would display the total of both products and lead to the checkout.

Here is some additional functionality, unrelated to the product selection, that I considered for the main screen:
- A **Help** dialogue including a support phone number and an email, since there is no human that operates the kiosk. This way customers will be able to get help and we could use it as an opportunity to learn how to improve the kiosk.
- **Bottle Ruler.** Some customers won't know how much liquid the bottle they brought can hold. To help them, we can create a 'ruler' with examples of bottles in different sizes that would match the

actual size of these bottles in real life. It won't be precise, but I believe it could be accurate enough to give an approximation of their bottle capacity.
- In the future, we could even create an effortless **Fill my bottle** experience. Once the bottle is placed on the shelf, a scanner would automatically measure it, suggest how much liquid it could hold, and automatically prefill this amount into the checkout.

Once the customer is finished adjusting their order and has pressed the "proceed to payment" button, we'd display instructions for payment methods (Illustration 3.7). I assume we want to have a direct billing relationship with the customer and not make them pay via the supermarket cash register. It would allow us to receive payments faster and make our kiosk operate as independently as possible. In this case, we'll request customers swipe their card in the card reader on the right. If the kiosk is connected to the internet we could accept PayPal, Bitcoin etc. but for the first version we could take cards only, since this payment method covers almost all of our customers. This way we could ship the product faster.

3.7

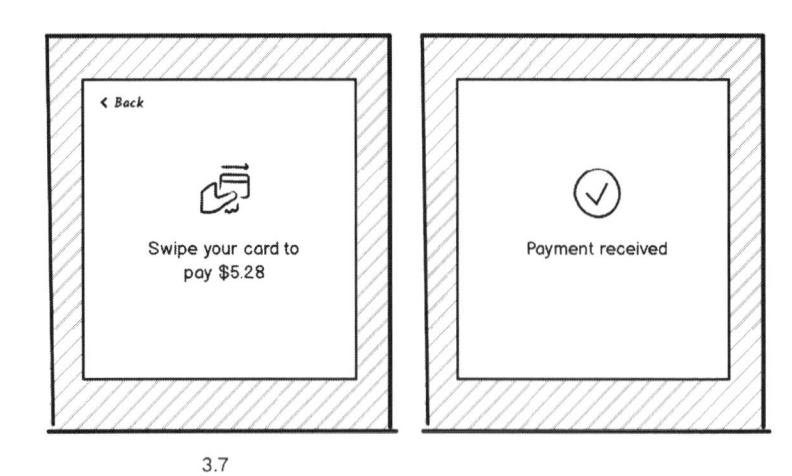

Illustration 3.7: Payment process

After completing the payment, the customer would be shown instructions about where to place the bottle and press the "Go" button to start the filling process (Illustration 3.8). A countdown would appear towards the end of the filling process (Illustration 3.9).

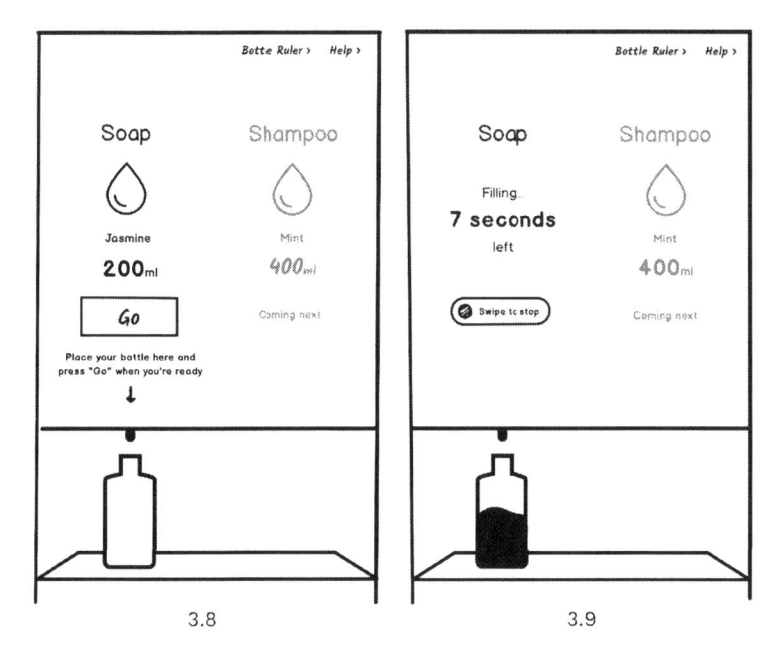

Illustration 3.8: Step after payment making sure the customer's bottle is placed ready for fillingt.
Illustration 3.9: Bottle filling in process.

On the final screen, after the transaction ends, we could display information about the resources the customer saved by choosing our products over bottled ones. For example "with this purchase you saved 4 litres of water that would have been used to produce a plastic bottle" or "...you saved $x vs. buying a bottled product". This would increase their awareness of the environmental impact of our product, make them feel good about their purchase and more likely to return.

Step 7: Measure success (How)

To measure the success of this interface and its future iterations, I'd track:
- First interaction count — how well does the default screen attract attention?
- Checkout completion time — how long does it take to finish the purchase?
- Checkout success rate — measure how many customers finish the checkout process.
- NPS (Net Promoter Score)

3.2. A self-publishing platform for Amazon

Task: 81% of Americans want to write a book[18]. In fact, 31% of all e-book sales in the Kindle store are of self-published e-books. Design a product for self-publishing a book on Amazon, decreasing the entry barrier to self-publishing.

This is an exercise with a large scope, so it would be most appropriate for a take-home exercise. It tests the candidate's ability to comprehend and map out a multi-step process that they are most probably unfamiliar with.

Since the product is supposed to be a part of Amazon, this is a great challenge for testing how the candidate deals with using an existing design system.

Step 1: Understand your goal (Why)

Amazon's mission is to build a place where people can find and discover anything they might want to buy online. Books are a huge part of Amazon's business, especially the Kindle store which is a high-margin product, since it doesn't require physical operations. By minimizing the entry barrier for book publishing, Amazon would increase the marketplace supply, and as a result, their revenue.

---

[18] "Think You Have a Book in You? Think Again" — New York Times
http://www.nytimes.com/2002/09/28/opinion/think-you-have-a-book-in-you-think-again.html

Amazon already has a product called Kindle Direct Publishing, but I'm not familiar with its interface and features so I believe that, to some degree, I'm going to redesign it during this task.

Step 2: Define the audience (Who)

People self-publishing a book are most probably:
- 30-80 years old
- Middle/Upper class
- Likely to be self-employed
- Highly educated

We can divide the product's audience into two main groups:
- First-time authors
- Recurring authors

Both have similar motivations, but slightly different needs. More guidance is needed for new authors and more efficiency is needed for recurring ones.

Step 3: Understand the customer's context (When/Where) and needs

While going through the self-publishing process, this is the usual **context** for authors:
- **When.** I assume customers start working with our product when they are already at an advanced stage of content writing, at which point they start checking what their publishing options are.
- **Where.** Authors write their books using their laptops, desktop computers and maybe tablets

from anywhere — home, coffee shops, co-working spaces, airports etc. I'd expect them to work on the publishing process with the same setup.
- **Feelings**. Excited, anxious. New authors might feel overwhelmed by aspects of publishing they weren't even aware of.

This is what the customer **needs** to self-publish a book:
- Cover design
- Editing of the manuscript
- Illustrations
- Content layout design
- Web presence
- Foreword written by a thought leader
- Different customer-ready formats for the e-book
- To set up hard-copy book production and shipping
- Marketing materials e.g. graphics, direct emails, a website
- To set up the finance e.g. royalties payments, taxes

Step 4: List ideas (What)

Book publishing involves a lot of aspects — working with manuscripts, graphics, communicating with vendors and more. I think building a web app allowing authors to work on these tasks from their laptop/desktop, as they are already used to, would provide them with the best experience.

The post-publishing experience could be more relevant for mobile, so authors can track their readers' statistics and payments on the go.

Step 5: Prioritize and choose an idea

We determined that we'll build a web app in the previous step, so we can skip this step.

Step 6: Solve

The product should have a dedicated area, disconnected from the Amazon marketplace, so authors will have as few distractions as possible while working on publishing their book. Although, to reduce the friction of creating a new account, authors should be able to login with their Amazon credentials (as it works with Audible today).

Our customers are either first-time authors and feel anxious or unclear about the process they are about to start on, or recurring authors publishing a new book. That's why the screen after login should be welcoming and friendly to make authors less anxious about the long and sometimes unclear path ahead of publishing a book. It should encourage them to add their first book to the app and start the self-publishing journey (illustration 3.10).

> | Amazon Direct Publishing   Dashooard   Books   Sales   🔔 ○
>
> ### Publish your book for millions of readers
>
> Amazon is here to help you with all you need to publish your book
>
> [Add Book ›]
>
> | 40m+ | $1k/mo | 50k |
> |---|---|---|
> | Monthly readers | Average revenue per author | Authors self-published |

Illustration 3.10: An after login welcome-screen.

Once the customer starts a new book flow, they will be taken, step-by-step through all the aspects of publishing we mapped in Step 3 (illustration 3.11). The process isn't necessarily linear, so they should be able to move between different steps and fill them out, gradually saving their process. For this kind of experience, I'd use a wizard-like experience with a master-detail layout.

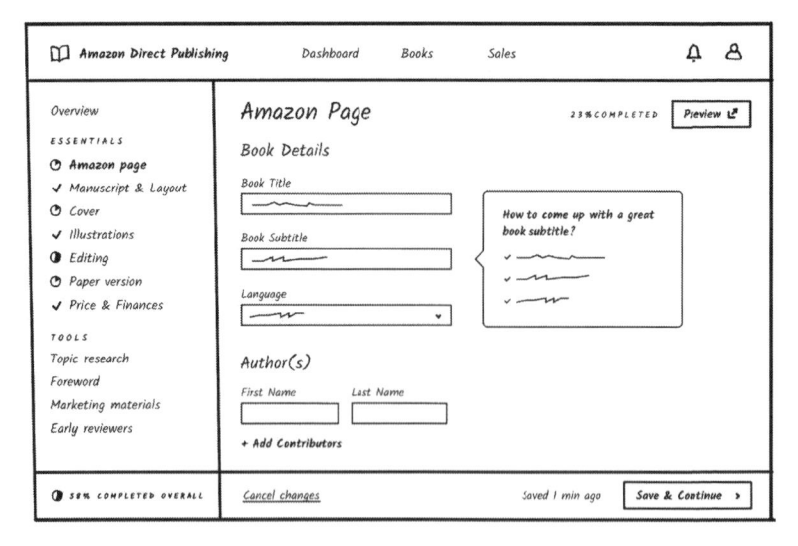

Illustration 3.11: Amazon page setup step.

The sidebar (master) would have two goals: navigation between publishing steps and providing feedback on the progress i.e. indicating how much of each step is completed. The latter would create a better understanding of the big picture and create a feeling of progress to motivate authors. A sidebar would also allow us the flexibility to adjust features of the publishing process without breaking the design layout.

To make the steps list less overwhelming and more scannable, I divided it into two categories:

- **Essentials** — steps required for publishing a book on Amazon
- **Tools** — "nice-to-have" services that help authors to produce a more successful book.

The sidebar sections would be:

- **Overview** — a book dashboard for keeping track of the publishing process, answering questions "What's my progress?" and "What's next?". For books recently added, the dashboard could begin by providing an overview of steps we recommend to start the process.
- **Amazon page** (3.11) — where the author can upload information needed to create a presence in the Amazon marketplace. This page would include a "Preview" option for imitating how the page would look when published on Amazon.
- **Manuscript & Layout** (3.12, 3.13) — book manuscript upload and setup/preview of how the book would look in digital and printed version.
- **Cover** (3.14) — a marketplace of designers who could provide illustration services for self-publishing authors. I believe Amazon could easily create a pool of freelance designers. The marketplace flow would help authors to prepare a brief for designers.
- **Illustrations** — a marketplace of designers. I'd assume it would be the same pool as for cover design.
- **Editing** — a marketplace of editors.
- **Paper version** — printing and shipping setup. Today Amazon produces books on-demand and handles the shipping, so in this section authors should be able to calculate the costs (paper type, book size etc.)
- **Price & Finances** (3.15) — setting up the book price and calculating royalty earnings.

- **Foreword** — a tool helping authors to commission a foreword. Forewords are usually written by established thought-leaders. Considering Amazon might have the biggest database of published authors, it could be a great platform for connecting well-established authors and newcomers.
- **Marketing materials** — guidelines and/or marketplace for producing graphic materials like a book blurb, banners, and website needed for the book's launch
- **Ask for a review** — reviews are one of the main purchase drivers on Amazon. I assume that launching a book with existing reviews would increase its chances of success. Amazon could connect active reviewers of similar books with authors before they launch the book. Authors could give away their book in exchange for a genuine review. This way, authors get early feedback, reviews for their Amazon book page, and a testimonial they could use on their website.

For the designers' and editors' marketplaces our product should ideally have a communication system between authors and vendors. Although, as an MVP, we could create a list of vetted vendors so authors can communicate with them directly.

While choosing the step in the sidebar, the content area (detail in master-detail) would display data inputs required for completing it. Some of the steps require similar types of interactions (filling out forms, uploading files, calculating costs, finding a vendor etc.) so we could create a design system of reusable components to make it easier to develop the product. Here are some building blocks that could be reused across the product:

- **Forms** (illustration 3.11) — probably the most commonly-used element for textual information input.
- **File upload** (illustrations 3.12, 3.13, 3.14) — manuscript or graphics for cover and illustrations.
- **Marketplace** (illustration 3.14) — any interaction with a third party i.e. finding a designer, editor or an author for a foreword.
- **Calculator** (illustration 3.15) — tools for understanding costs for printing, shipping and potential royalty earnings.
- **Preview** — a representation of the data in some other context: preview of the book layout in the printed/digital version or the book's web page on Amazon.

After creating these building blocks, we can reuse them in our product adjusting for each of the use-cases.

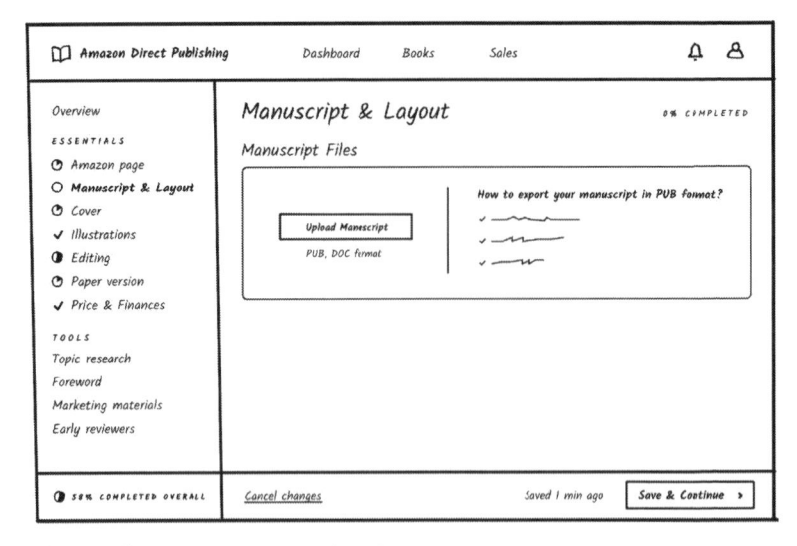

Illustration 3.12: Manuscript & Layout setup empty state.

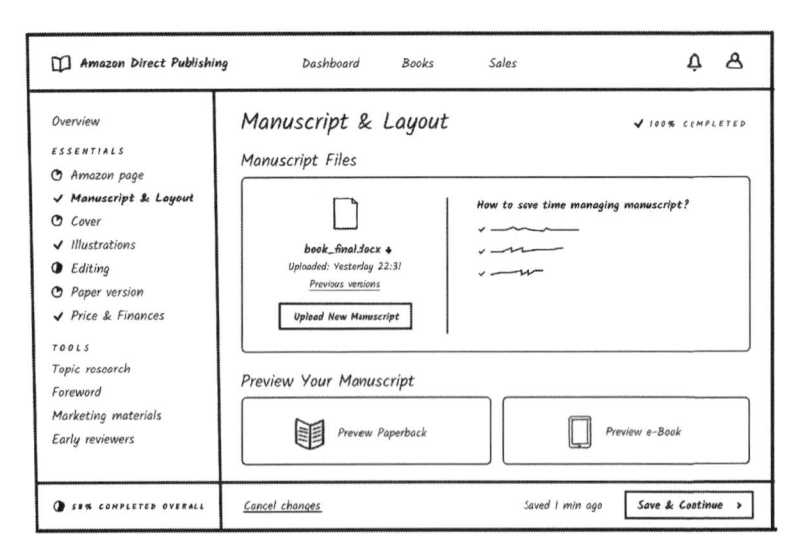

Illustration 3.13: Manuscript & Layout setup after user uploads their manuscript.

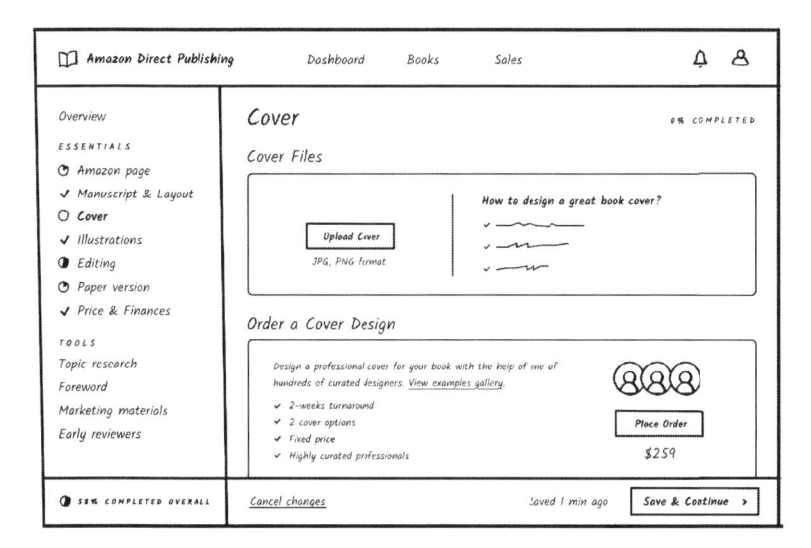

Illustration 3.14: Book cover step empty state with promotion of an internal designers' marketplace.

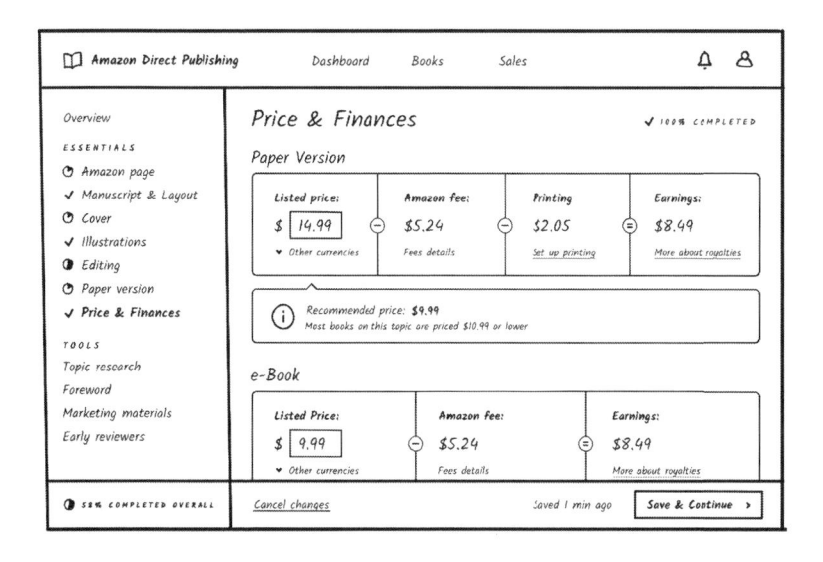

79

Illustration 3.15: Price & Finances step with a calculator of final earnings for paper and digital versions of the book.

To reduce the pressure on the customer of constantly having to save their progress, we should auto-save all the data changed unless the user chooses "Cancel changes". Once the customer is finished filling out all the essential information, a prominent suggestion to proceed and publish the book will appear in the sidebar (illustration 3.16).

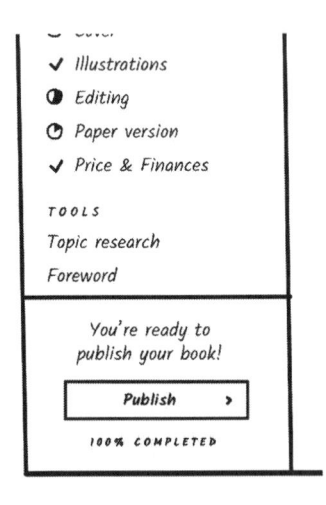

Illustration 3.16: Call-to-action area appearing once author has filled all required information for publishing the book.

Once the book is published, we should celebrate such a big milestone for the author and make them feel good about finishing this long process. The next natural step for them would be to preview how the book looks on Amazon and Kindle stores and start promoting their book — via social networks or using paid ads on Amazon (illustration 3.17).

Illustration 3.17: Success screen after author has completed the process and published their book.

One of the things we could leverage in this product is the data Amazon already has about the features which successful books have in common. This could help us to develop best practice guidelines for each aspect of publishing. For example, Amazon could determine, from their sales data and reviews, if using illustrations makes non-fiction books more successful. If there appears to be a correlation, they could suggest authors include illustrations. Readers would therefore receive a better product and both the authors and Amazon would become more successful.

Step 7: Measure success (How)

Assuming we're redesigning an existing product, I'd compare the metrics of the old design with the new one:
- Overall completion rate — % of books that finished the process of publishing from all books added to the product.
- Completion rate of each step.

Both of these metrics bring authors closer to publishing a book which would make Amazon's business more successful.

In addition, I'd measure features retention. For example, if authors use our marketplace of designers but choose not to do that again for their next book, there is a chance their initial experience with the marketplace wasn't positive.

3.3. A dashboard for freelancers

Task: Design a business management dashboard for a freelancer.

In this challenge, the candidate is requested to design a single aspect of a product, while the audience is clearly defined. This means that the candidate will be able to focus more of their time on the solution instead of exploring different audiences and ideas on how to serve them. This task could be used for a live whiteboarding session or an on-site exercise.

Another aspect that makes this exercise relatively easy is that it doesn't require the candidate to showcase a flow, but only a product in a static state. If you want to practice designing a full flow, you can use slightly different phrasing: "Design a project management app for a freelancer". This way it can be also be used for a take-home exercise.

Here is a good example of an interviewer-interviewee interaction to begin this challenge:

Interviewer: We want you to design a business management dashboard for a freelancer.

Candidate: Great, can I assume we're designing the dashboard for a web app?

Interviewer: Only if you think it makes sense.

Step 1: Understand your goal (Why)

The global workforce is becoming more independent, so the market of freelancers is going to grow constantly in the next few years. People dream about the independence and flexibility freelancing provides, but they don't always realise how much administration it requires.

Building a product that simplifies the administration of freelance business would help freelancers to spend more time on the actual work and to become more successful. It is a service that freelancers would be happy to pay for since it directly affects their income. In addition, I believe it could reduce the entry barrier to becoming a freelancer and, in that way, increase our potential market.

Step 2: Define the audience (Who)

Here are three classifications I think will help us to define different groups of freelancers that have different needs:

Their profession:
- Designers
- Developers
- Writers
- Photographers
- Videographers
- Marketers
- etc.

Freelance work arrangement type:
- Full-time
- Part-time
- Retainer contract

Prior freelance experience:
- New to freelancing
- Already freelancing

Step 3: Understand the customer's context (When/Where) and needs

When. We're going to connect with our customers (the freelancer) at almost every step of their business operations. At each step they could feel differently — excited to issue a proposal to a potential client, happy that they won a new client, annoyed that they are cancelling an invoice. We could communicate differently with them at each of these steps to cheer them up or to celebrate when needed, thereby providing a human touch.

Where. Freelancers spend most of their work time in front of their computer in various places — at home, in coffee shops, co-working spaces, airports etc. Some of the professions we mentioned, like photographers or videographers, spend a lot of time "in the field" so, I assume, they would appreciate the flexibility of being able to manage their business on the go from their smartphone as well.

Needs. The main need we're addressing with our product, and specifically the dashboard, is to enable freelancers to be in control of their business. To do that, I believe these are the questions freelancers should be able to answer when using our product:
- How is my business doing financially?
- How should I plan my future work?

- What can I do now to move my business forward?

Step 4: List ideas (What)

As the professionals we listed earlier spend most of their working time on their computer, I believe our core product should be a web app. It would meet them where they already are and provide the best experience for managing their business. This app should also provide a mobile experience, enabling customers to be updated on their business status and perform actions on the go.

Step 5: Prioritize and choose an idea

We have already determined what we are building in the previous step.

Step 6: Solve

The dashboard is the main entry point to the app and I believe has two main goals:
- Informational (providing an overview of business performance) and
- Navigational (providing quick access to the app's main areas and actions).

I believe the informational goal could be achieved by fulfilling the needs we discovered earlier:
- *How is my business doing financially?* Providing financial status
- *How should I plan my future work?* Providing projects' status
- *What can I do now to move my business forward?* Suggested action items

I'd build our dashboard to have three content parts dedicated for each of these aspects (illustration 3.18). I'd put the projects area first, since they drive freelancers' everyday work. The action items area could be empty, at various points, so I'd give it the least prominent area on the page.

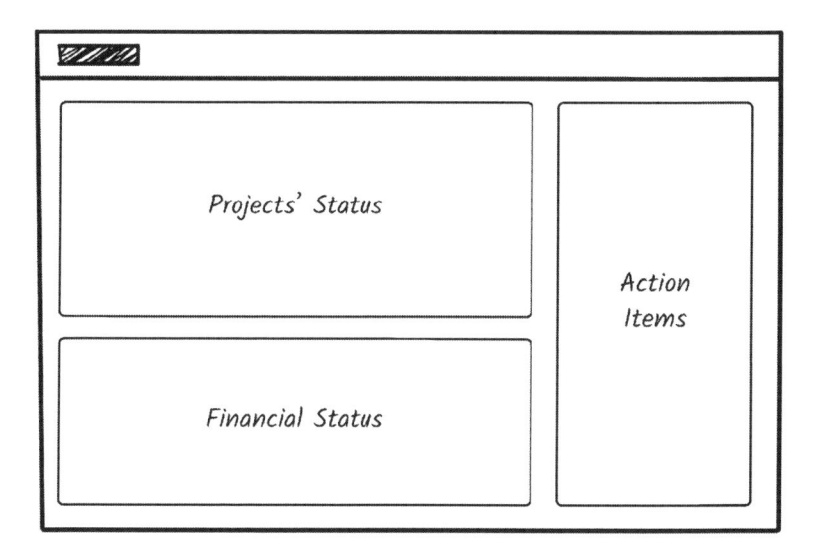

Illustration 3.18: Dashboard content areas.

To better understand the information each of these parts and the navigation should include, I'll map out a freelancer's workflow of managing a project.

I'll start with the navigation (illustration 3.19). First of all, everything in a freelancer's workflow is related to a specific client and project. These are two main building blocks essential for anything a freelancer does, so I'd allow quick access to projects and clients.

The eventual goal of a freelancer is to finish a project and get paid. To do that, they need to go through this cycle:
- Issue a proposal
- Issue a contract
- Track time
- Track expenses
- Issue invoice
- Receive/track payment

I believe that freelancers would need to access each of these aspects often across their clients or projects (e.g. to see all the payments or proposals issued recently). To make them easily accessible from anywhere in the app, I'd use them as part of primary navigation. It's a long list that won't fit in the header, so we could include them as a vertical list of items in a sidebar as part of a master-detail layout.

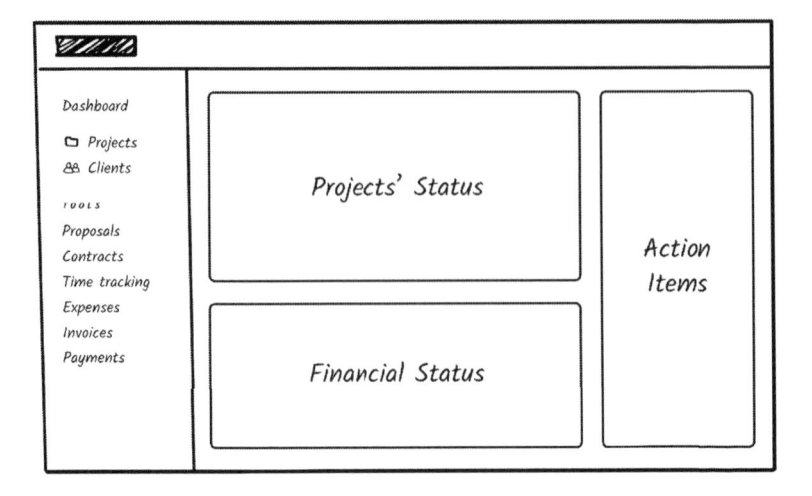

Illustration 3.19: Master-detail layout for our dashboard with sidebar navigation.

Now, when we're done with the navigation, let's go back to the content part of the dashboard and understand what content it should include (illustration 3.20):

- **Financial status.** I believe freelancers want to answer two main questions to understand how their business is doing financially:
    - *How am I doing?* To answer that question, we could display all finance-related numbers relevant to the current month: outstanding payments, payments made, expenses, overdue payments. Each of these metrics should also link to the relevant parts of the product.
    - *Am I getting better?* Show the current month's statistics in relation to the previous month and a projection for the next month. We can use a graph to represent these comparisons using three key metrics that will communicate the bottom line: Paid, Expenses, Profit.
- **Projects' Status**. Previously we mapped out the full project cycle — from issuing a proposal to receiving a payment. Since these steps are chronological, we could place each project on a timeline which will provide an overview of where they stand and what the freelancer should do next.
- **Action Items**. Updates list with suggested next steps that could be taken to move the project forward. For example, to follow up with a client on

a contract that was issued a week ago but hasn't yet been signed, or to do a client-requested update to a proposal.

There are two features that could be relevant to the customer, regardless of which screen they are on: the "Start Timer" and 'Search'. To make them accessible from anywhere in the app, I'd place them in the header.

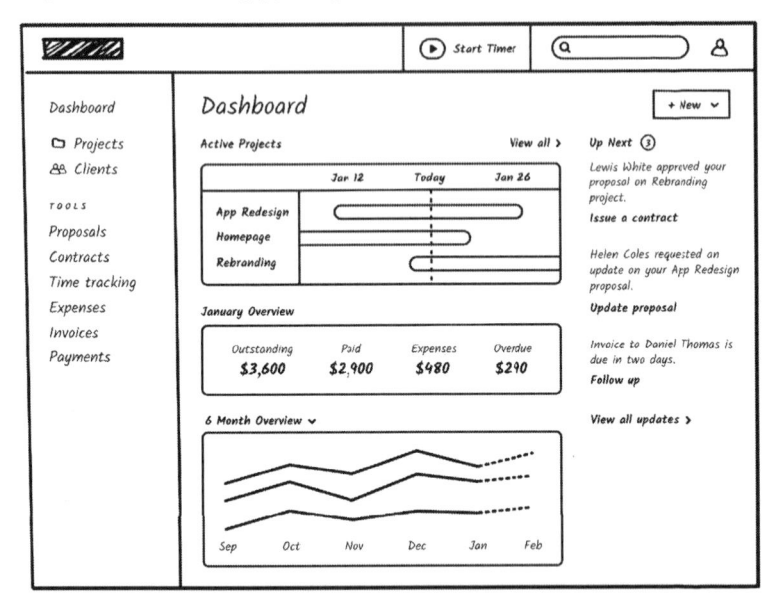

Illustration 3.20: Dashboard with three content parts: financial status, projects' status and action items.

In addition, the dashboard could be used to provide quick access to the most common actions for creating new items (illustration 3.21):
- Proposal
- Expense
- Invoice

- Contract
- Project
- Client

```
+ New ⌄
┌─────────────┐
│ Proposal    │
│ Expense     │
│ Invoice     │
│ Contract    │
│ Project     │
│ Client      │
└─────────────┘
```

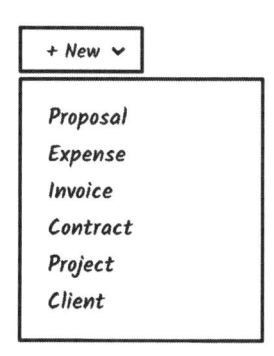

Illustration 3.21: Call-to-action button drop-down with quick access to main features.

For the mobile version, I'd reorganize the content by (Illustration 3.22):

- Minimizing the navigation to a hamburger menu. Even though a hamburger menu usually undermines navigation discoverability, I believe it's an appropriate solution since it will still expose the actions customers are most likely to perform when on mobile.
- Creating a separate tab for "Up Next". This way, we can make the updates counter visible and prominent at the very top of the screen. By grabbing the customer's attention, we can provide them with any important updates on their business status with a glance.

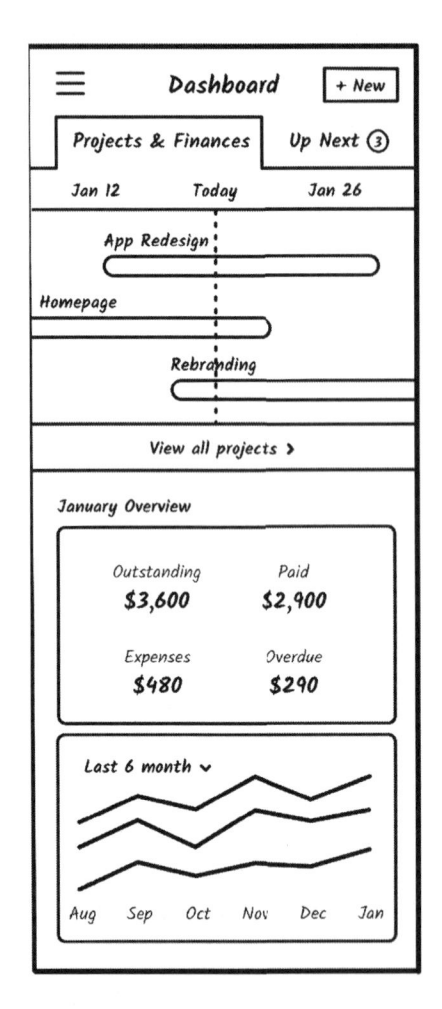

Illustration 3.22: Mobile version of the dashboard

When I think about specific freelance audiences that could be served uniquely, here are some that come to mind:
- New freelancers could be given guidance on setting up their business and issuing their first contract or invoice.

- Practicing freelancers could be given advice on how to import their data from the tools that they used previously.
- Retainer contractors normally have a constant client, project and income, so the kind of dashboard we designed won't be very valuable for them. I ignored this audience for this exercise since they are a minority, but in the final product we could devise a way to specially cater for this audience.

Step 7: Measure (How)

- "Up next" actions completion rate — it would validate that we successfully provided a way to quickly move forward a freelancer's projects and business.
- Run a survey on the dashboard before and after the launch of this design and ask customers to respond to these statements on a scale from strongly disagree to strongly agree:
    - *This app helps me to understand how my business is doing financially.*
    - *This app helps me to understand how I should plan my future work.*
    - *This app helps me to understand what I can do now to move my business forward.*

'The dashboard will affect the key metrics of the product as a whole, so the key performance indicators of the product itself would provide useful tools for measuring its success. Here is a list of some product metrics I thought of:

- Project completion rate
- Freelancer's growth (they earn more)
- Retention over time
- Engagement (defined actions performance rate)
- NPS

3.4. Improving primary health care

Task: Primary care is associated with enhanced access to healthcare services, better health outcomes and fewer people going to hospital. It is also correlated with more equitable distribution of healthcare within a population. Today the US healthcare system faces a significant shortage and inequitable distribution in the primary care workforce. Design a digital product to make primary care more accessible.

This challenge can be tackled with a variety of different products for different audiences. The task can be used for any type of challenge — a whiteboarding session, an on-site challenge or a take-home exercise.

To ensure that the suggested solution covers all of the challenge types, I made it detailed enough for a take-home exercise. So, for the whiteboarding session and on-site challenge, a less detailed solution would normally be expected.

***

Step 1: Understand your goal (Why)

Primary care plays a key role in public health. General practitioners are the gatekeepers of medicine and serve as first tier support in the case of an existing condition or prevention of future diseases. By spending more time with more patients, GPs could prevent serious problems, some of which could even be lethal in the long-term, such as cancer, stroke and heart disease.

By creating more opportunities for patients and primary care professionals to spend time together, we could improve people's quality of life, save lives and, I assume, billions to the healthcare system.

Step 2: Define the audience (Who)

Key audiences we could build products for are clinics' personnel and patients:
- General practitioners
- Nurses
- Clinic receptionists
- Patients

From this list, I'd focus on two groups:
- **Patients** since they are the main audience who eventually we want to serve better.
- **General practitioners** whose time is the most expensive resource of all clinic personnel. By optimising it, we could make the most significant impact on increasing access to general care.

Step 3: Understand the customer's context (When/Where) and needs

The interaction between patient and healthcare system is usually initiated by the patient, when they have a health concern or a problem. So, we'll explore the experience from a patient's perspective, although we'll keep in mind that for prevention we might need clinics to be more proactive.

Patients' context:
- Time: interaction with the clinic starts with the patient not feeling well, which can happen any time of the day or week.
- Location: patients schedule an appointment from home, work or on the go. The next step would usually be physically going to the clinic, checking in at reception, sitting in a waiting room and meeting the doctor in their office.
- Emotion: Feeling anxious, uncertain.

The basic need of a patient using a clinic's services is usually to get treatment from a professional that is:
- High quality
- Familiar
- Affordable
- Nearby
- Has a low wait time
- Has a convenient appointment time

Here are some user stories based on the context and the needs we explored above:
- As a patient, I want to know if my appointment is covered by my insurance or, if not, how much it would cost, so I can understand if it's a good option financially.
- As a patient, I want to make sure I find a good doctor, so that I am confident they will help me with my condition.

- As a patient, I want to schedule my appointment as soon as possible so that, if my condition needs urgent treatment, it doesn't get any worse.
- As a patient, I want to make sure the doctor can see me at a time convenient to me, so that I don't need to be absent from work.
- As a patient, I want to spend the least time possible in the clinic, so that I am less likely to catch other people's illnesses.
- As a patient, I want to know if there is anything I can do before seeing the doctor, so that I can attempt to improve my condition.
- As a patient, I want to make sure I remember to convey all the relevant information about my condition to the doctor, so that they have the necessary details and context to give me the right treatment.
- As a patient, I want to know what my condition is as soon as possible to avoid unnecessary anxiety.

I think it could be beneficial to map out the most popular reasons for patients to go to a clinic. I assume they would be:
- Prescription renewal
- General check-up
- Irregular blood pressure
- Getting a sick note for their employer
- Back pain
- Mental health
- Diabetes
- Vaccination

We can see that many of the conditions listed here are preventable, which we should take into consideration in our solutions.

Step 4: List ideas (What)

1. **Family doctors' marketplace** — a website and mobile app for finding a general practitioner nearby where you can see their reviews, ratings and prices.
2. **Doctor advice via an on-demand platform** — text or video chat with a doctor on-demand from your computer or smartphone, available at any time and from anywhere. It could be either an independent product or a white label for clinics.
3. **Shared appointments via video** — giving a shared economy angle to primary care. Build a mobile app connecting GPs and groups of patients who have common, preventable conditions that are either newly developed or ongoing. GPs could arrange group appointments on issues like lower back pain, diabetes, skin diseases, mental health, quitting smoking etc. It would make appointments cheaper, more accessible and hopefully prevent diseases requiring future, more expensive, treatment. It could be either a white label platform for clinics or an independent platform.
4. **Improved appointment scheduling system for clinics**. It would allow the patient to list their reasons for setting an appointment in advance and possibly:
    - re-route issues that could be treated by nurses to save GPs' time.

- provide GPs with advance information they would normally ask for face-to-face, with any problematic answers flagged.
- provide self-treatment information that could improve the patient's condition prior the appointment.

Step 5: Prioritize and choose an idea

I'll place potential solutions on an Impact/Effort matrix to assess their feasibility (illustration 3.18). Solutions #1 and #2 already exist to some extent and are relatively easy to build. However, they have low impact as does #4, which also suffers from being harder to implement.

I believe that the #3 has the biggest impact, even though an innovative concept like this would likely require a lot of effort to implement. I'd go with this idea, since such a product doesn't exist yet and we could create a new market where we could have the advantage of being the first player.

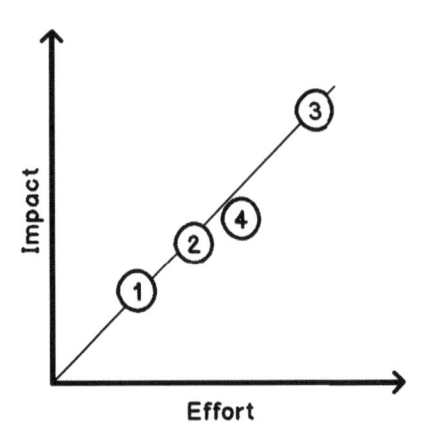

Illustration 3.18: Impact/Effort matrix of ideas we mapped in Step 4.

Step 6: Solve

I will make the assumption that doctors explain the same things about the same conditions to different people multiple times a week. This process could be optimised by grouping these patients, connecting them with a doctor who will talk about the condition, and having a group discussion afterwards. Allowing patients to join the group remotely via a smartphone would make the entry barrier low, by reducing the required commitment and effort to attend in person.

Shared appointments already exist. Around 10% of family physicians in the US give patients the option to share their appointments with people who have similar health issues. What we're going to build is a white label product that allows clinics to organise group appointments for their patients and start practicing this concept.

For the sake of the exercise, I'll show the experience from the patient's perspective even though our product will obviously be used by GPs as well. To start building the app UI flow, I'll map user-tasks that explain the steps patients should take to use our app successfully:

- Open the app
- Log in with your clinic credentials
- Choose an appointment type
- See time slots available
- Choose the convenient slot
- Pay

- Get a notification about the appointment starting soon
- Open the app
- Join the appointment
- (optional) Request to ask a question
    - If the doctor approves the request, join the call to ask a question.

Once the patient opens the app, the first screen should communicate what this app is about, probably including an explanatory video, and reinforce the service's value propositions (illustration 3.19):
- Save time and money
- Prevent future diseases
- Learn from other patients participating in discussions.

Patients should be able to login with the same credentials they use to access their usual clinic's services online. If they don't have login credentials, patients would be able to create an account or join the clinic membership.

After authorisation, the main screen would suggest to the patient the most relevant appointments (illustration 3.20). By building a white label product for clinics, we'll have a privilege of access to patients' medical data, so we can use it to suggest relevant appointments based on:
- **GP advice**. E.g. During a face-to-face appointment, the GP diagnoses depression and advises the patient to join a group appointment to help educate them about their condition.

- **Existing conditions**. E.g. A patient with a history of back pain complaints will automatically be offered participation in a pain management group.
- **Risk factors**. E.g. A patient who is obese, over 40 and has high blood pressure is in a high risk of having diabetes[19]. Someone with these risk factors may automatically be recommended to participate in a prophylactic appointment for diabetes prevention.

3.19

3.20

---

[19] "Diabetes - Symptoms and causes - Mayo Clinic." 31 Jul. 2014, https://www.mayoclinic.org/diseases-conditions/diabetes/symptoms-causes/syc-20371444.

Illustration 3.19: Login screen for patients with value propositions of the product.
Illustration 3.20: Main screen with a list of suggested patient appointments.

Each item in the appointment types list would include information for patients so they can decide if it fits their:
- Schedule (appointment duration).
- Condition (recently diagnosed/ongoing treatment/prophylactic).
- Budget (appointment participation price).

On the appointment screen, the patient could get more information about what to expect from the appointment, the benefits of participating and view a list of available time-slots (illustration 3.21).

After choosing a time-slot, the patient would be asked to approve the payment (Illustration 3.22). Since the clinic already has the patient's details, the payment can be processed seamlessly and appear on their monthly clinic bill. Even though this payment type is an advantage, I'd add an explanation for the patient, since payment is a sensitive step that needs to be very clear.

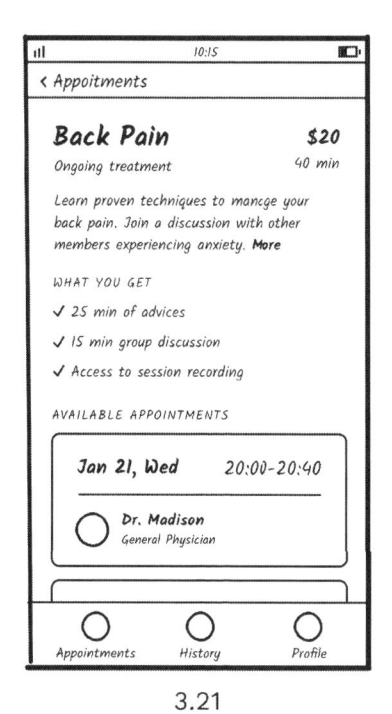

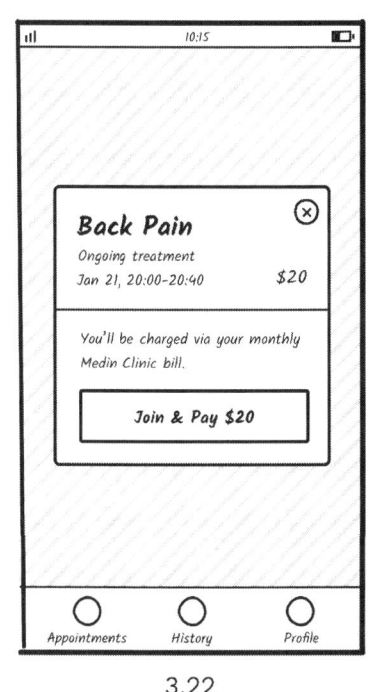

Illustration 3.21: Appointment details with a list of time slots available for this type of appointment.
Illustration 3.22: Modal window for appointment approval.

Once the appointment is scheduled we could suggest setting up a reminder, using their preferred method, to make sure they won't miss it i.e. Calendar, SMS, push notification etc. (illustration 3.23).

Now, once the appointment is scheduled, it will be prominently displayed on the home screen to make sure the patient remembers it and has quick access to the appointment information. The app would send a push notification with a reminder 30 minutes before the appointment and at the time it starts.

Illustration 3.23: Post-schedule screen with suggestion to set up an appointment reminder.
Illustration 3.24: Homescreen shortly before an appointment begins.

Once the patient joins the streaming of the appointment, they'll see the video with an option to signal to the doctor that they have a question. If the doctor approves their request to join the discussion, the app will signal to the patient that they can join. The experience during the call is similar to most video-call interfaces with options to mute, hang up and disable the video (illustration 3.25).

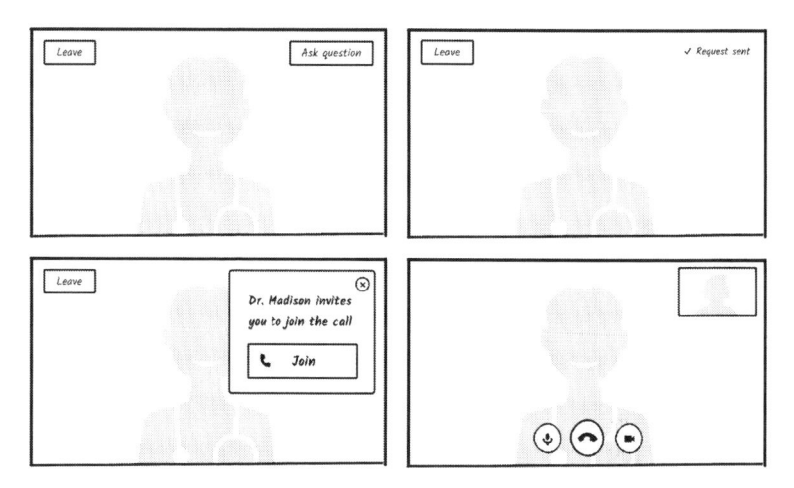

Illustration 3.25: The appointment experience – watching the streamed video call and asking a question.

After the appointment ends, the patient will see a summary screen with instructions on how to access the recording and an option to find a follow-up appointment (illustration 3.26).

Illustration 3.26: Appointment end screen.

Step 7: Measure success (How)

To measure the success of our app in enabling customers to participate group appointments, I'd measure:
- Appointment sign-ups conversion
- Discussion call-in requests rate
- Appointments attendance rate

These are the business metrics I'd measure to validate the success of the concept of group appointments:
- Percentage increase of patients who saw a doctor this month

- (Long-term) Whether patients who participated in an appointment on disease prevention are less likely to have this disease
- (Long-term) Whether patients spend less money on their health care, while retaining a similar or higher level of health.
- (Long-term) Whether clinic spends less money per patient, without decreasing the quality of service.

Canvas

You can find an example of how the framework canvas (see Appendix) can be used in solving this exercise here: http://productdesigninterview.com/canvas-healthcare.

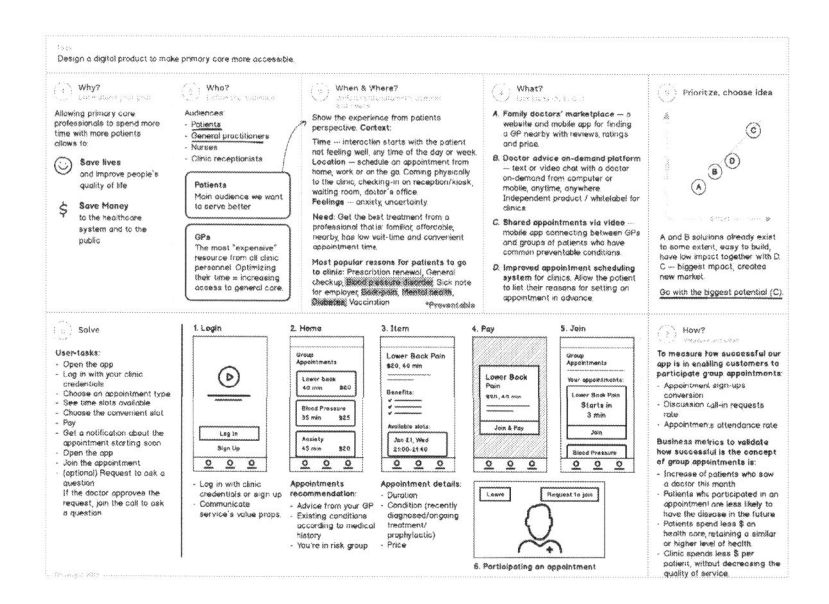

3.5. Improving the ATM experience

Task: Improve the ATM experience.

This is a great exercise for a live whiteboarding session. The task is phrased in broad language to test how the candidate narrows down the problem. It can be taken in different directions, depending on both candidate and interviewer — from redesigning the way people interact with financial services or redesigning just the ATM UI. I have suggested a solution that is somewhere in the middle.

Here is an example of a good interviewer-interviewee interaction to begin this challenge:

Interviewer: We want you to improve the ATM experience.

Candidate: Would you like me to focus on the experience of using an ATM we're familiar with today or should I rethink the whole concept of how people interact with their bank to perform financial operations?

Interviewer: Let's focus on the ATM experience as we're familiar with it today.

Candidate: Great, should I focus on a specific type of ATM? For instance, those installed in bank branches or third-party ATMs we see in convenience stores?

Interviewer: Let's explore the kind that is owned by a bank and either mounted on a wall on the street or inside bank branches.

Step 1: Understand your goal (Why)

I believe that, even though the ATM is a great piece of technology, the experience of using it has barely changed since it was invented. By improving it we could:
- Deliver a better financial service to customers.
- Make them more likely to use our bank ATMs.
- Make them more loyal to our bank.
- Expand our services to under-served groups.

All of these could result in increased revenue for our bank.

Step 2: Define the audience (Who)

People using ATMs belong to:
- All age groups starting, I assume, at 13 (when teenagers use their parents' prepaid or credit cards).
- All social classes, apart from extremely low-income citizens. I assume we're focusing on ATMs used in developed countries, where the majority of people from all social classes have debit/credit cards.

When I think about more specific groups who might need a separate or unique approach, here are some that come to mind:
- **Senior citizens** sometimes left under-served by digital products, because they have low tech-savviness. Lowering the entry-barrier for senior citizens using our ATM could make our product more appealing to them.

- **Tourists / immigrants** probably want to use the ATM in their native language so they can better understand the exchange rate and any fees incurred.
- **Teenagers** start interacting with money much earlier than they are legally allowed to have a bank account. I believe there is an opportunity to create solutions to serve their needs and educate them about finance.
- **The disabled**. I'm not sure how easily blind people or those with motor conditions are able to use ATMs. I assume they can be better served.

Step 3: Understand the customer's context (When/Where) and needs

When thinking of the customer **context** in relation to ATMs, these things come to mind:
- A public place.
- During the day and night.
- Noise on the street.
- A range of weather such as rain or snow, bright sunlight.
- A potential queue.
- Feeling unsafe / suspicious.

The **needs** a customer has while using the ATM may be:
- Withdrawing cash (I'd assume 80% of ATM usage).
- Paying bills i.e. utilities, phone bills etc.
- Depositing cheques or cash.
- Printing bank statements.
- Transferring money.
- Checking the balance.

- Other financial services.

We can see that some of the needs don't really require an ATM and could be performed on the bank's website or via a mobile app. We'll try to keep this in mind while thinking about solutions.

I believe there are some sub-optimal conditions for using ATMs today that we have an opportunity to improve:
- Touching a dirty keyboard and screen.
- Waiting in a queue.
- Card fraud risk.
- Requirement to own a credit and debit card.
- Requirement to have the card with you.
- Remembering the PIN code.
- Lack of accessibility to customers with disabilities.

Step 4: List ideas (What)

When I think about possible improvements for ATMs, here are some ideas that come to mind:

1. **Interface redesign.** Build a clearer and more efficient interface, so we can reduce lines, usage errors and the time spent by customers using the ATM.
2. **Cardless identification.** Build fingerprint/face/smartphone recognition into ATMs to remove the entry-barrier of owning or carrying a card for using ATM services. For customers who already have a card, it would also become unnecessary to remember the PIN code.
3. **Converting the ATM to a cash/deposit/printing point.** ATMs would only be required for the final step of "physical" transaction i.e. collecting the

cash or printed statements, depositing cheques etc. All the requests could be made via smartphone beforehand.
4. **Mobile app for children/teenagers.** This would allow parents to give prepaid credits to their children for withdrawing via ATM and educate them about finance. This would introduce a new audience to the ATM.

Step 5: Prioritise and choose an idea

I'll place the ideas onan Impact/Effort matrix to assess their feasibility (illustration 3.27). The interface redesign (#1) is the quickest improvement we could ship. I like #2 and #3 because they make owning a card unnecessary for using an ATM. It might not be in the bank's interests today, but it would definitely improve the customer experience and differentiate the bank from competitors. It also reduces the risks of card fraud, which is good for both customers and banks.

I'm not sure about the regulatory aspect of idea #4, which might prove challenging, so I'd probably avoid using this idea.

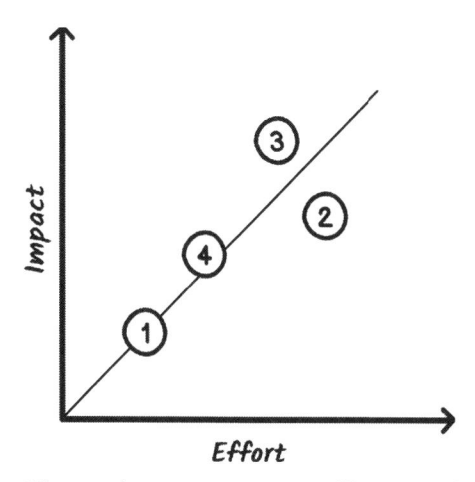

Illustration 3.27: Impact/Effort matrix of ideas we mapped in Step 4.

#3 has the biggest impact, since it has several advantages. It removes the need for owning or carrying a card, minimises interactions with the ATM, reduces queues, makes the ATM more accessible and reduces card fraud. This is the idea I would pursue.

Step 6: Solve

Firstly, the solution we have chosen is about suggesting a way to enhance the existing ATM experience, rather than replacing the way they are used today (at least not immediately).

Let me create a quick storyboard explaining how I see the user experience (Illustration 3.28).

1. Create a request via smartphone

2. Approach/ navigate to ATM

3. Identification with smartphone

4. Collect or deposit goods

Illustration 3.28: Storyboard showing the ATM being used as a cash/deposit/printing point.

Most banks already have mobile apps that allow their customers to perform financial operations. Requesting operations with ATMs could be part of these apps. Here is the list of "physical" operations that could be requested on mobile and performed on ATM:

- Withdrawing cash
- Depositing cheques and cash
- Printing bank statements

We could create entry points to this experience from the relevant parts of the app. For example, the account statement can have a "Print" button that allows the customer to use a printer connected to the Wi-Fi network or an ATM to print it.

In addition, these use-cases should get one dedicated area (for example "ATM" tab) in the mobile app, since for most customers these operations will still be associated with an ATM (illustration 3.29).

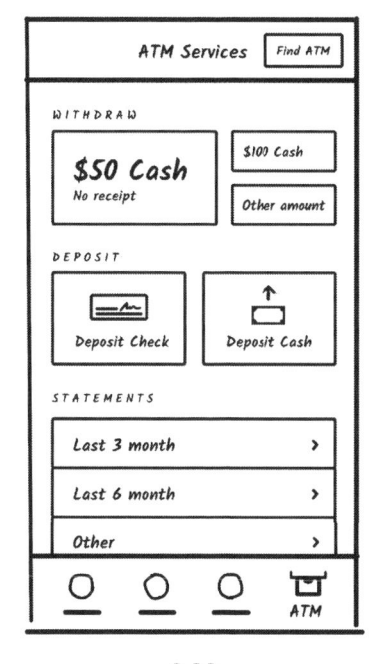

Illustration 3.29: Dedicated area for ATM operations in the bank mobile app.
Illustration 3.30: Code scanner for connecting the app to the ATM.

Over time, we can learn about the customer's habits and adjust this screen accordingly. For example, I assume most people withdraw the same amount of cash most of the time. So, on this screen we could suggest quick access to withdrawing this amount.

Ideally, we would prefer customers to perform the action on their smartphones in advance to minimise their time in front of the ATM and reduce the queue (illustration 3.30). When requests are "Saved for later", the app will send a push notification once the customer is near to a bank's ATM (illustration 3.31). In addition, to provide quick access to the request, it will appear in the bank's app widget and in the app itself (illustration 3.32).

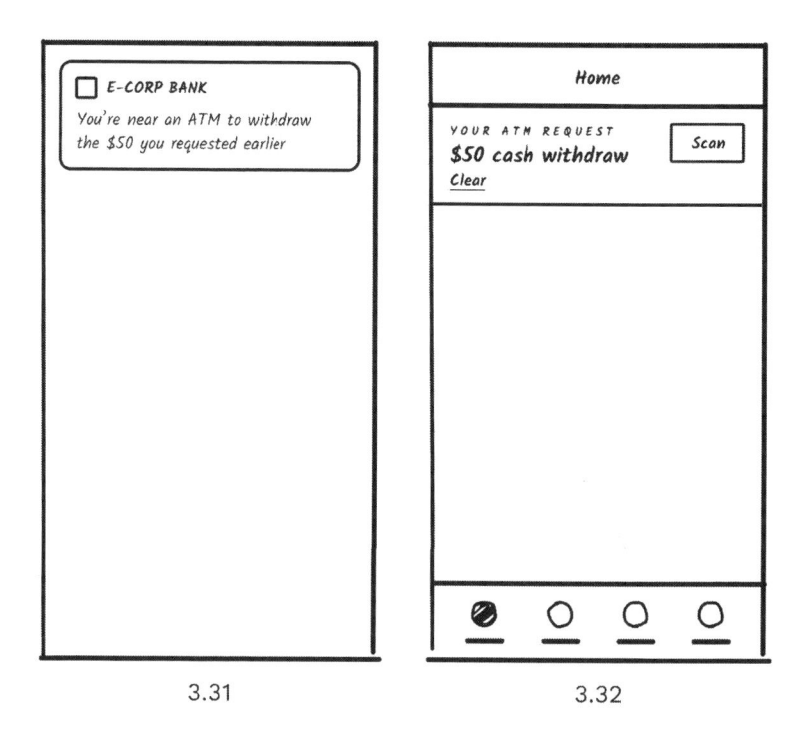

[Figure 3.31: Mobile notification showing "E-CORP BANK — You're near an ATM to withdraw the $50 you requested earlier"]

[Figure 3.32: Home screen showing "YOUR ATM REQUEST — $50 cash withdraw — Clear" with a Scan button]

3.31   3.32

Illustration 3.31: Notification about saved action when an ATM is located nearby.
Illustration 3.32: A quick access to the saved action banner on the homescreen.

Our ATM machines will have a QR code that creates a handshake between mobile and ATM, sending the request to the ATM (illustration 3.33 and 3.34). At this point, the ATM will change its language according to the customer's smartphone language. After waiting for the ATM to process the request, all that is left is to collect or deposit the physical goods (illustration 3.35).

3.33　　　　　　　　　　3.34

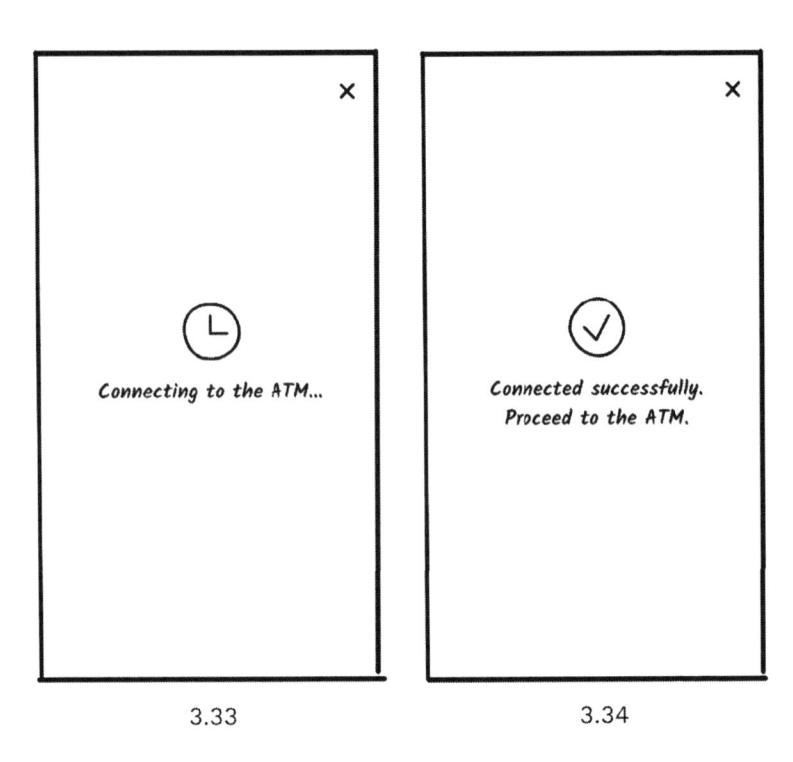

Illustrations 3.33, 3.34: Mobile app connecting to the ATM after scanning the QR code.

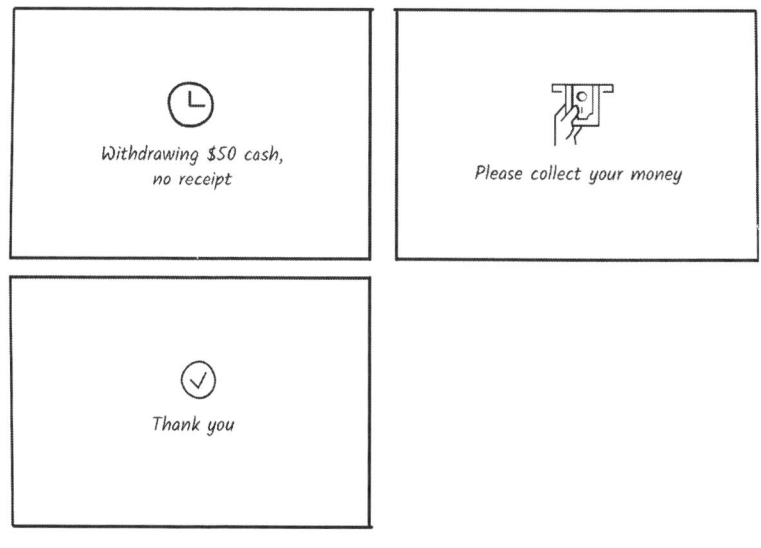

Illustration 3.35: ATM screen after receiving the cash withdrawal request.

Mobile operation systems have built-in support of accessibility features such as voice-over and increase of font size. Thus, I believe that this solution will automatically make the ATM experience more accessible, just by allowing customers to perform requests via their smartphone instead of using an ATM's screen and buttons.

Step 7: Measure success (How)

Here are the metrics I'd measure in order to understand if our redesign was successful:
- Churn rate — % customers who try the new experience but return to using the ATM interface afterwards.
- Reduction in ATM queues.

- Decrease in requests to restore PINs.
- Reduction in card fraud.
- Adoption rate by people with disabilities.

Chapter 4
How to use a design exercise when interviewing

The first thing you should understand before giving a candidate design exercises is **what skills you are trying to test**. To do that, you should consider these two questions:
- What skills does the candidate need to be successful at your company?
- What skills are you less confident the candidate has?

In my team at WeWork, we sometimes asked design candidates to perform two tasks — a take-home exercise focused on visuals/UI and an on-site exercise testing product thinking. To optimise the hiring funnel we started with the exercise we were less confident the candidate had appropriate skills for. In this way, candidates could be omitted earlier in the process by testing their weaknesses first. I found the technique of using two exercises testing different perspectives very useful and efficient, and I would recommend it. Just make sure your hiring process doesn't become too long and exhausting for the candidate. If you have additional evaluation steps, like a portfolio presentation or design critique, then it's worth thinking about this.

Candidates more likely lacking product thinking skills	On-site exercise Testing product thinking	Take home exercise Testing visual/UI skills
Candidates more likely lacking visual/UI skills	Take home exercise Testing visual/UI skills	On-site exercise Testing product thinking

Illustration 4.1: Exercises for discovering candidates' weak points early in the process.

Take-home exercise

For junior positions, you want to test a candidate's visual skills and ability to produce deliverables, ready for development, using appropriate tools. For this purpose, you can use a take-home exercise with a deadline of two to seven days, making sure the candidate is aware that you'll send them the task with this deadline. A general guideline is to spend four to eight hours in total on the task.

In choosing what kind of exercise to give candidates, think about the type of work they are being hired for. If you run a SaaS system you most probably want to give them a task of designing a dashboard and not a marketing landing page. Here is an example for a take-home task:

Design a landing page for a marketplace you wish existed (including a mobile version). If you have time, design flow of purchasing on the marketplace.

Present your solution using any medium you wish – a keynote presentation, an interactive prototype or JPGs.

If possible, provide a Sketch file that developers would potentially be able to start working with right away.

When interviewing a remote candidate, you can ask them to implement this kind of task and present it via video-call afterwards.

Keep in mind that using take-home exercises alone won't allow you to evaluate skills mentioned in Chapter 1 such as communication, critical thinking, the ability to ask questions, handling feedback and criticism, performance in a high-pressure environment. Similarly, it won't tell you whether they are the kind of person the team would like to collaborate with on a day-to-day basis.

On-site exercise

To test the candidate's product thinking you could either use a live whiteboarding session or give the candidate time to think about the solution in a quiet room for an hour and present their ideas afterwards.

I believe that, even though live whiteboarding tests the skills a designer should have for the job, these kind of tasks should be used primarily for senior positions and for first design hire. Some designers need more quiet time to think about solutions and could feel under pressure while solving an unfamiliar problem in front of a stranger.

The discussion should cover the solution(s), the thought process, and any other open ideas that weren't explored. Here are some guidelines that will help you to perform a successful on-site interview:

- Make sure you have made the logistics of the interview clear and that the candidate feels comfortable. Offer them a drink and provide them with markers, papers and pens, and sticky notes.
- Solving a problem in a short amount of time and presenting it to strangers is hard, especially if the candidate is not used to it or didn't have the chance to do this in their previous job. Try to make the candidate feel comfortable. Be friendly and empathetic.
- If the candidate gets stuck, try to help them. Remind them that the exercise is not about a single detail and don't make them feel trapped.
- Try one pushback during the interview or presentation to see how candidate reacts.

Here are some useful questions to ask yourself about the candidate during and after the interview to help summarise their evaluation:
- Do they ask questions?
- Can they take feedback well?
- Do they communicate clearly? Are they easy to talk to?
- Do they follow a process or jump straight to the solution?

- Have they made valid assumptions?
- Do they talk about how their solution connects to the company's mission?
- Do they think about the target audience?
- Do they relate to the users' context and define their needs?
- How do they decide which solution is the best?
- Do they talk about both the strong and weak sides of their solutions?
- Are they exploring solutions beyond the obvious ones?
- Do they set goals for measuring the success of the product and their design?

How to come up with an idea for a task

Here are some tips to help you come up with an idea for a task:

- **Look for a market opportunity**. Find a market that has an obvious business opportunity. It can be a market you're familiar with or one you research. Ask the candidate to come up with a product creating value in this market.
    - Example: Pet care is a $60 billion market. Think about a product that could capitalise on demand for these kinds of services.
- **Find problems that need to be solved**. Think about what problems are out there. If you can't think of one, you can find some here:
    - Go to CNN.com, skim over the headlines and find a problem that people are having, which can be solved with a digital product.

- Go to Product Hunt[20], and reverse engineer the problems some of the products try to tackle.
    - Use the IdeasWatch[21] website, a community where people share and discuss startup ideas, to find problems they are attempting to solve.
- **Look at established companies' business needs**. Pick a company and suggest the candidate explores its business opportunities which could be solved with a digital product. Alternatively, suggest they improve a specific business-metric i.e. redesign [product/feature] to improve [metric]
    - Example: Pick a target user who you don't feel is well served by Spotify. How would you redesign Spotify to appeal to them?.

You can find plenty of examples of exercises in Chapter 5.

Why companies shouldn't use tasks based on their own products

Companies still use their own product challenges as exercises to test design candidates. It's the easy thing to do, since there is no need to invent a new problem. I believe it is not a good practice for three reasons:

- The interviewer is going to have so much more context and knowledge about this problem than the

---

[20] "Product Hunt." https://www.producthunt.com/.

[21] "IdeasWatch." Startup inspiration from the crowd http://www.ideaswatch.com/.

candidate, making it very hard for them to approach its result objectively.
- The interviewer will be swayed by their own thinking on the product. Daniel Burka, a design partner at Google Ventures, put it this way: "You're also heavily biased towards decisions that you helped make [...] In the end, you will choose the candidate who just happens to try solutions that align with your perspective[22]."
- It's ethically wrong. Solving the existing problems of the company during an interview could feel like a free consultation, especially if the company is not compensating candidates for their time.

I believe giving candidates exercises related to your products will do more harm than good for you and your business. So, my advice is to avoid it.

---

[22] "Stop asking design candidates to redesign your product. It's unfair and ...." 29 Sep. 2014, https://medium.com/startup-grind/dont-fool-yourself-testing-job-applicants-on-your-own-product-is-unethical-and-ineffective-8ac6affd73a7.

Chapter 5
Tasks list

A collated list of all tasks mentioned in the book

Design a landing page for a physical product that costs more than $200.

***

LinkedIn decided to build a marketplace for freelancers. Design a flow for hiring a professional.

***

Build a desktop app dashboard for a general practice doctor.

***

Pick an under-served audience by Spotify. Suggest how they could improve their offering to this group.

***

The NYC MetroCard system has remained unchanged for decades. The cost of the MetroCard machine infrastructure, the time lost waiting in line to buy a MetroCard, touching a dirty machine to do it, the potential of losing the MetroCard, and the ease of gaming the system by swiping your card for others has cost the city millions of dollars and leaves much to be desired from the user experience.

Design a new system that allows someone who uses the metro every day, or an-out-of-town visitor who will use the metro just once, to access the metro on time, without having a physical NYC MetroCard to hand.

Constraint: Every suggested technology has to be available on the market today.

***

A few trends of note: 54% of the world's population live in urban communities, the average marriage age for men is 29 (up from 26 two decades ago) and for women is 27 (up from 23 in the same time period). Given these trends, city dwellers tend to spend most of their twenties living with roommates. Finding and keeping a good roommate, however, gets harder as more and more people live in cities.

Design a mobile product experience that appeals to millennials and that makes it safe to find the ideal roommate in New York City. Design the experience from the perspective of a person who is looking for a roommate, as well as the one who is looking for the apartment. Once the ideal roommate is found, what else can this product do to improve the roommate experience?
We are looking for you to identify and solve the problems in the finding and keeping a good roommate journey...

Constraint: Stick to the existing mobile capabilities of iOS and Android.

***

Redesign Waze to support bike rides.

***

Improve the Spotify mobile experience.

***

Design a product to improve freelancers' workflow.

***

Design a restaurant reservations management platform.

***

Design a product that creates a new revenue driver for Airbnb.

***

Improve Pinterest's retention.

***

Design an ATM machine for children.

***

Design an alarm clock for the blind.

***

Redesign Spotify to better serve parents with children.

***

Design a shared queue feature for Spotify. It should allow the user to listen to music curated by a group of friends.

***

Design a kiosk for liquid soap and shampoo refill.

***

81% of Americans want to write a book[23]. In fact, 31% of all e-book sales in the Kindle store are of self-published e-books. Design a product for self-publishing a book on Amazon, decreasing the entry barrier to self-publishing.

***

Design a business management dashboard for a freelancer.

***

Primary care is associated with enhanced access to healthcare services, better health outcomes and fewer people going to hospital. It is also correlated with more equitable distribution of healthcare within a population. Today the US healthcare system faces a significant shortage and inequitable distribution in the primary care workforce. Design a digital product to make primary care more accessible.

***

Improve the ATM experience.

---

[23] "Think You Have a Book in You? Think Again" — New York Times
http://www.nytimes.com/2002/09/28/opinion/think-you-have-a-book-in-you-think-again.html

Additional tasks

Pick a target user who you don't feel is well served by Amazon.com. How would you redesign Amazon.com to appeal to them?

***

Pet care is a $60 billion market. Think of a product that could capitalise on the demand for these kinds of services.

***

Today, 54% of the world's population lives in urban areas, a proportion that is expected to increase to 66% by 2050. Projections show that urbanisation,, combined with the overall growth of the world's population, could add another 2.5 billion people to urban populations by 2050. Think about a digital product that could help governments and municipalities dealing with this challenge.

***

On average, a typical middle class American family wastes more than 4 million lbs of materials. The majority of that is what they throw away or recycle on a daily basis. How can Americans be more conscious about the waste they throw away?

Assume technology can play a role in helping here. Give the user an interface that can help them manage their waste disposal. Feel free to be imaginative with the potential of how hardware and software can integrate to solve the problem.

Constraint: Suggested technology should either exist today or should be viable for the market within six months.

***

Gary is a Gen-Xer, still a young 30-something bachelor, college educated and accomplished in the tech field. On a recent trip to his general physician, he was diagnosed with early signs of obesity.

Design the lowest barrier to entry flow using any device(s) that makes Gary want to track his daily food intake and intervene when he shows signs of over-eating. His life depends on it.

Constraint: All technologies and suggestions must be viable for use today.

***

Valentina leads sales and business development for a Fortune 500 company. She travels three out of four weeks in the month, and when she travels, it's almost always internationally. Between all her travel to different time zones and a busy meeting schedule in different cities, she finds it challenging to keep up with her calendar and to show up in the right places at the right time.

Design a calendar flow and interface that is smart enough to suggest meeting times, accounts for changing time zones, and is proactively working for Valentina to make sure she is always on time for her meetings.

Constraint: the solution has to be mobile-friendly and has to use currently viable technologies.

***

Audiobooks and podcasts are the fastest growing audio segments on mobile. Users who listen to audiobooks don't enjoy the benefits of touching pages, highlighting excerpts or leaving notes on their favorite pages. They also lose the nostalgic aspects of owning a book and watching it age. This leaves a lot to be desired from the audio experience on mobile.

Design an audiobook or podcast mobile app that is highly personal, highly interactive and with the ability to bring even more utility to the user than a book ever could.

Constraint: All suggested technologies need to exist, or should realistically exist within the next six months.

***

Spotify has decided to give artists control of their catalogues on their platform. For the first time, artists can manage their own albums, upload their own artwork, sell specific merchandise, add lyrics to their music and it's all on their own terms.

Design a Mac-based editor and artist management system that allows artists to manage their presence on Spotify. The solution should account for all of the artist's existing content on Spotify, but feel free to get creative and add additional features that an artist might find useful.

Constraint: You are designing a Mac-based desktop app so you will be constrained by the OS's abilities, but you can disregard any web-related technical constraints because they don't apply here.

***

You are consulting Google on an important strategic decision for their enterprise offerings; they want to know whether it's worth introducing a sales funnel management tool in to their Enterprise Gmail interface.

Google believes that because a majority of their Enterprise users discuss business on their email platform, and that is where most people have their business contacts stored, that they are in a position to both make the sales process more efficient and make the likelihood of closing business deals higher.

26% of Google's Enterprise users engage in sales weekly, 40% engage in some sort of funnel management (whether sales, hiring, or some other decision funnel).

A typical sales funnel includes leads, inquiries, prospects, quotes and finally a new customer.

Recommend a funnel management flow to Google. Make sure the flow accounts for a user making initial contact with a lead from within Gmail and then managing that lead through the entire funnel. What else can Gmail do to put the odds of closing business deals in favour of their user?

***

Design a mobile app for yoga teachers to manage their customers.

***

Design a product that allows gym trainers to create a workout plan for their clients.

***

Design a feature for Airbnb, allowing a group of friends to plan and book their mutual vacation.

***

Build a product helping people to relocate to a new country.

***

Design the UI of the screens on the back of airplane seats.

Chapter 6
Interviews

I interviewed five design leaders who provided a lot of useful insights about different aspects of their design careers. The interviews are below.

Bobby Ghoshal: how designers should change their mindset

Bobby Ghoshal is a co-founder of Candid Co and a co-host of the High Resolution video series. For the series, he interviewed 24 design executives at companies like Airbnb, Spotify, Facebook, Slack and Uber to discuss how they approach, communicate and deploy design. Prior to that, Bobby served as Head of Design and Growth at WeWork.

Q: Bobby, based on your personal experience and what you have learned from the interviews, what is the one skill designers should be improving and why?

A: The long road to design-relevance at your company is paved with bricks of business awareness; designers need to understand business now. I strongly believe that designers with business sensibilities are primed to own the future of our industry. The TL;DR of it is, we need to mature from user experience designers working only on product problems to customer experience designers who frame the entire customer journey to increase the likelihood of "selling" someone on our product.

So many of the designers I speak to are overly concerned with specializing in visual design, motion design, website design, wireframing... you name it. We're seeing a Cambrian explosion of design tools that are helping us get so good at this stuff that bad design can easily masquerade as good design these days. Though that isn't really the hard work, that's the fun work. We spend all our time having so much fun focused on the perfect product experience that we've lost touch with what really matters... the customer. We forget *(or don't realize)* that most people who consider our product **never actually become a customer** and in turn don't experience our product.

Businesses lose on the order of 90-95% of people to poor pricing, poor reviews, misinformed brand positioning, poor marketing, poor operations, and poor customer service. These are all design problems, all of them. Every person in marketing, operations, finance, and support are making customer experience decisions every day and effect, in a very real way, how prospective customers see your product and company. Using the design process to push the needle in the right direction on all those fronts is the biggest and clearest opportunity I see for designers right now.

By no means am I suggesting that marketing, finance, and operations fall under the auspices of design; though, as designers we are in a position to influence these kinds of decisions internally at our companies. The next decade of design leaders will need to recognize the importance of building influence in their companies by spending a bulk of their time away from their desk and building diplomatic bridges with teams that are directly affecting the entire customer experience and not just with teams affecting the in-product user experience.

This means we're going to need to get comfortable with talking about business strategy, understanding margins, getting dirt under our fingernails digging through conversion metrics on all channels, listening in on customer support calls and finding pressure points that could help inform our marketing etc. These are areas we're not too adept in today.

The mindset change from being a "user experience designer" to a "customer experience designer" may seem small, it isn't. It will change how your company sees you, how your customers see your company, it will yield a higher value transfer to both your company and the customer and is the surest way to get massive business buy-in for precious company money to get re-invested into design.

Justin Maxwell: advice for designers who want to become founders

Justin Maxwell has been a designer, manager, and PM for Apple, Google, Sony, and many startups, most notably Mint.com (acquired by Intuit). Three years ago Justin founded Smith.ai (https://smith.ai) where he currently serves as Chief Design Officer.

Q: Justin, you've worked for some of the best tech companies in the world and eventually founded your own business. There are many designers who aspire to build their own company one day. What skills should they work on to prepare for that day while still being employees?

A: There are 1,000 things, but ultimately they roll up to three main categories: discipline, people skills, and big-picture thinking. I have focused on things you can practice (or impose on others) in an "employee" environment safely.

"Discipline" is the hardest for me because I, like many folks, continually succeed through my procrastination. However, discipline applies to everything from alignment to key principles and OKRs to chasing shiny things that might make you feel successful but don't move the needle. When you are an employee, it is easy to rely on the constraints others (or organizations) set for you to force discipline, but when you are building your own company, you are responsible for constant organizational alignment to your own constraints and objectives. Start with B.J. Fogg's "Tiny Habits" practice and build the neural pathways for discipline, so it comes naturally when others depend on you for it. Within this bucket you can also find organization, prioritization, focusing (anti-distraction), fitness, and health & hygiene.

"People skills" is a broad category, but the ultimate goal is facilitation in achieving your objectives through others. Negotiation (seek out Stuart Diamond's "Getting More" courses) will likely be the most frequently used skill in daily life, professional and personal. Presentation and storytelling skills align others with your vision, whether that is a new feature or a VC pitch. While one cannot accelerate management experience, they can likely build strength in active listening, critical inquiry, hiring & interviewing, sales, and pitching, in their current roles. Building up armor (dropping the ego) from the process of selling and being rejected helps in every interaction from hiring through landing customers. It may seem obvious, but if you are not a reliable communicator in text or speech, fix that immediately, or, at least, use Grammarly before sending emails to people.

Lastly, "Big-Picture Thinking" is the heart of OKRs and principled thinking — terms that are thrown around but rarely practiced correctly. Despite your years of Dribbble posts and trendy typographical choices, the design of your company's product or service must satisfy user need, before anything else. Unless cosmetic appeal is your single differentiator in a crowded market, it is time to get comfy with the bare minimum. Big-picture thinking as a company leader means you choose words carefully, spend dollars wisely, triage product decisions deliberately, and seek opportunities that get you closer to the goals you have set.

And as any company founder will tell you, I wish that I could adhere to that above advice 100% of the time, but the last skill should be this: get comfortable with chaos.

Helen Tran: the skill most designers overlook

Helen Tran is a product designer living in Toronto. She was at Shopify for four years, the last two of which she was a Design Lead, building up a team of 30 designers. While being at Shopify she also designed the Toronto office's internship program for product designers. Recently, Helen made a shift to working on her own software product, in addition to mentoring product designers on the side.

Q: Helen, you've had the chance to meet a lot of design candidates while building your team at Shopify and now through your mentoring program. What is one skill that designers you've met tend to overlook which consequently prevents them from growing or getting hired? Do you have tips on how they could learn and practice this skill?

A: A designer's job is certainly to help build the product or feature, but a large part of their job is to ensure that what everyone is building is the right thing for the user. If a designer can't explain to me the bridge between the business needs and the user needs, I know they haven't really done their research.

When a designer is handed a target market, they typically trust the people who gave them the directive that their assumptions are correct. Except they usually aren't, and they're typically steeped in someone else's biases. A designer should always be doing thorough research to double-check assumptions and ensure that the team isn't going to be investing their time into making something nobody needs or wants (those are two different things.)

There are practical deliverables: user experience/service/journey mapping, running design sprints, and in-depth market interviews that can be done. With those deliverables, leadership and soft skills are needed to present to the team and encourage them to build what makes the most sense for both the business and user.

The practical deliverables can always be practiced through repetition, but so can the soft skills. Get the team involved in doing group critiques, participate in more company speaking opportunities, and run group retrospective activities. If you're a freelancer, join Toastmaster groups, improv groups, or social groups that meet often. Try your best to go beyond the tech scene and practice in other groups.

Challenge your bubble. If it's uncomfortable, it's a good sign.

Joel Califa: two tips for getting a job

Joel Califa is a Senior Product Designer at GitHub. Previously, he led product design at DigitalOcean, where he built the design team from the ground up.

Q: Joel, you've been on both sides — as a hiring manager and recently as an interview candidate, ending up at GitHub. What tips could you give to designers who are looking for their next full-time job?

A: The main piece of advice I usually give is to treat getting a job like you would a design process. You are the product and the hiring manager is the user. You want them to have a great experience and to buy what you're selling. That means they very quickly need to understand who you are, what you can do for them, and decide that it lines up with what they need.

To do that, you need to do a good deal of research. There are a lot of questions you can ask that could give you an edge over other candidates. For instance, who is this hiring manager and what do they believe in? You have access to their personal sites, Twitter history and comment history on certain sites. What does their team believe in? What kind of people have they hired in the past? What does the job posting require? What kind of language is used? What's the culture like? All of this data can inform how you go about differentiating yourself, how to frame yourself and highlight skills, which channels you should use to apply, what your cover letter should say, etc. It'll also give you a much better idea of whether the role is a good fit for you.

You should do this research separately for every new position you apply for, and customise the way you apply. 'Spray and pray' doesn't work for the jobs you want. When I was a hiring manager, I looked at dozens, maybe hundreds of CVs and portfolios a week. I developed habits, an eye for patterns, as well as a good amount of pet peeves. You want your first impression to be as perfect as it can be, and that takes work. It means polishing every single aspect of your application. Make sure it's well-designed. Make sure there aren't any typos. You want to distill your message and make the hiring team want to see more of you.

The second piece of advice is to learn to network. That doesn't mean going to a meet-up and exchanging your business card with every other person. It means following design circles you find interesting, and reaching out to people you like. The key thing people get wrong is treating these like exchanges and not real relationships. If someone is interesting to you genuinely try to get to know them. You'll likely end up with a new friend. Try to help people whenever possible, without expecting anything in return, and be nice to everyone. I attribute most of my success to just... being this way. Do this for a few years and you'll know everyone you need to know. It's much easier to get in the door and, more importantly, much easier to get the job, when people know you and your reputation. It won't get you the job if you don't have the required skills, but it can make a world of difference.

The bottom line is this stuff takes a lot of time and effort. Do the work, and you'll end up better off than where you started.

Mia Blume: skills which future design managers should work on

Mia Blume is the founder and CEO of Design Dept. A former design leader at Pinterest, Square, and IDEO, Mia started Design Dept. in 2016 to help transform the way creative leaders work. In 2017, she launched Within, a series of leadership retreats for women in design.

Q: Mia, at some point during their career, every designer asks herself if she wants to grow as an individual contributor or move to the management path. You managed designers at product companies and an agency. Now you run a company that educates designers on how to become managers. From your experience, what is one skill many designers who aspire to lead a team are usually lacking? How can they practice it?

A: I believe designers, unlike other fields in tech, bring some of the most essential skills from years of honing their craft to business leadership. This includes: creativity, vision, storytelling, empathy and systems thinking.

However, that doesn't mean they're always set up for success from the start. One of the most important things for designers to embrace when shifting to management is learning to let go of control and become a coach.

Over the years, we become astute at solving common design problems. However, it's unlikely that a designer spends any time teaching others to navigate these same challenges. So when an individual contributor shifts into management, the initial inclination is to tell their team how to solve their problems their way.

A few tips to get started:
- Stay focused on listening. They may approach you seeking an answer, but the first and most important skill of coaching is listening.
- Ask good questions that flip the problem solving back on your teammate, like "What's the goal of this exercise?" or "If you had two more weeks, how would you prioritize the work?"
- If you don't have to make a decision or direct a solution (e.g. high risk project or tight deadline), empower them to solve it themselves. Say explicitly that you trust their ability to navigate this challenge, and you're here to provide support along the way.
- If they ask for your opinion, offer it, but empower them to make the decision with the best information at hand. Also offer to brainstorm alternatives with them, or connect them with others throughout the organization that might have a unique perspective on the challenge.

Additional Resources

The interview process

Top 10 interview questions and the best answers. Many designers I spoke with during my research for this book said that they are intimidated by behavioural questions, like "What is your greatest strength?" or "Describe a stressful situation at work and how you handled it". Luckily, these questions aren't unique to design interviews, so there is a lot of content available on how to handle them well. My main advice is to prepare for these questions in advance so that you can progress to the stage of design exercises. This resource is a good start.
thebalance.com/top-interview-questions-and-best-answers-2061225

How to do a product critique is a guide for performing the product critique step of the interview by Julie Zhuo, VP of Design at Facebook.
medium.com/the-year-of-the-looking-glass/how-to-do-a-product-critique-98b657050638

10 questions you'll be asked in a UX interview is a list of crucial questions Ian Schoen (Senior Product Designer at SalesForce) was asked during his job search. Based on his experience of more than 40 coffee dates, phone calls, design presentations and one-on-one interviews.
medium.com/salesforce-ux/10-questions-youll-be-asked-in-a-ux-interview-f93f0c78f31d

How to build a UX portfolio if I have never worked in UX?
Fabricio Teixeira (Creative Director at R/GA) suggests five ways for solving the chicken-and-egg problem of needing a portfolio to get hired, but not being able to build one without being hired.
uxdesign.cc/how-to-build-a-ux-portfolio-if-i-have-never-worked-in-ux-80ebab8f3407

Learning product design and UX

High Resolution is a series of limited video-podcasts that includes interviews with design leaders from companies like Airbnb, Uber, Spotify, Facebook, Google IDEO, Instagram and Slack etc. Hosts Bobby Ghoshal (an interview with whom you can find in this book) and Jared Erondu discuss with their guests how their companies approach, communicate and deploy design.
highresolution.design

Case Study Club collects case studies about how digital products are built from all over the web.
casestudy.club

DesignBetter.Co is a learning hub built by InVision. It includes four free online books, providing 101 iproduct design principles, design thinking, design leadership and design systems.
designbetter.co

Nielsen Norman Group is one of the most reliable and in-depth resources about user experience. The organisation is

a consulting firm that shares research it conducts and produces free educational material..
nngroup.com/articles/

Career advice

How They Got There by Khoi Vinh, Director of Product Design, Mobile at Adobe, co-founder of Mixel, design director for The New York Times. This book is a collection of interviews with digital designers about their career, featuring Dan Cederholm (co-founder of Dribbble), Geoff Teehan (co-founder of Teehan+Lax, currently Product Design Director at Facebook), Evan Sharp (co-founder of Pinterest), Marcos Weskamp (Head of Design at Flipboard) and more.
howtheygotthere.com

Design Founders is a collection of interviews with the world's most successful designers-turned-entrepreneurs, who share their personal stories and the lessons learned along the way. The book features interviews with Ybes Behar (fuseproject), Evan Sharp (Pinterest), Scott Belsky (Behance), Zach Klein (Vimeo), Jeff Veen (Typekit) and more.
designerfounders.com

The Beginning of your Design Career is a short but on-point piece about 3-steps of a design career by Julie Zhuo.
medium.com/the-year-of-the-looking-glass/the-beginning-of-your-design-career-549828025494

Hiring designers

Crafting the Product Design Hiring Experience at BuzzFeed, by Sabrina Majeed, is a series of three articles about BuzzFeed's hiring process. It explores steps from sourcing candidates to onboarding a new design hire. In addition, BuzzFeed shared their designers titles and leveling here: github.com/buzzfeed/design. I really hope to see more companies follow BuzzFeed's example, in making their hiring process more transparent, so designers and other businesses can learn from it.
tech.buzzfeed.com/@sabrina

How to hire designers by Paul Adams, VP of Product at Intercom, maps out four skills against which businesses should be testing their design candidates.
blog.intercom.com/how-to-hire-designers

Khosla Ventures is a VC-firm based in California which built this thorough resource about hiring designers in tech..It helps those hiring to better understand how to evaluate UX skills, write a job description, source candidates interview them and more.
khoslaventures.com/resources/design-ux

Your Job Ad: The Start of a Great Hiring Experience, by Jared Spool, is a great article about how to write an effective job ad that will increase applications. I also recommend watching Jared's interview about creating the hiring process here: youtube.com/watch?v=6kDPodOOxLU.
articles.uie.com/job_ad/

The impact of design

In addition to the skills-oriented materials, I suggest you to check out these four resources which discuss the impact of design.

Offscreen Magazine is a print-magazine that asks critical questions about how we shape technology and how technology shapes us.
offscreenmag.com

Ends.: Why we overlook endings for humans, products, services and digital. And why we shouldn't is a book by Joe Macleod (former Head of Design at Ustwo). The book explores how we, as designers and consumers, overlook product endings, how it negatively affects the world and how we can fix that.
closureexperiences.com

SustainableUX is a free online conference for product-professionals who want to make a positive impact, on climate change, social equality, and inclusion, through their work.
sustainableux.com

Tragic Design is a book by Jonathan Shariat and Cynthia Savard Saucier. It explores how poorly designed products can anger, sadden, exclude, and even kill people who use them, even though the designers responsible certainly didn't intend any harm. The book teaches us how to avoid these kinds of mistakes..
tragicdesign.com

Appendix: Design Exercise Canvas

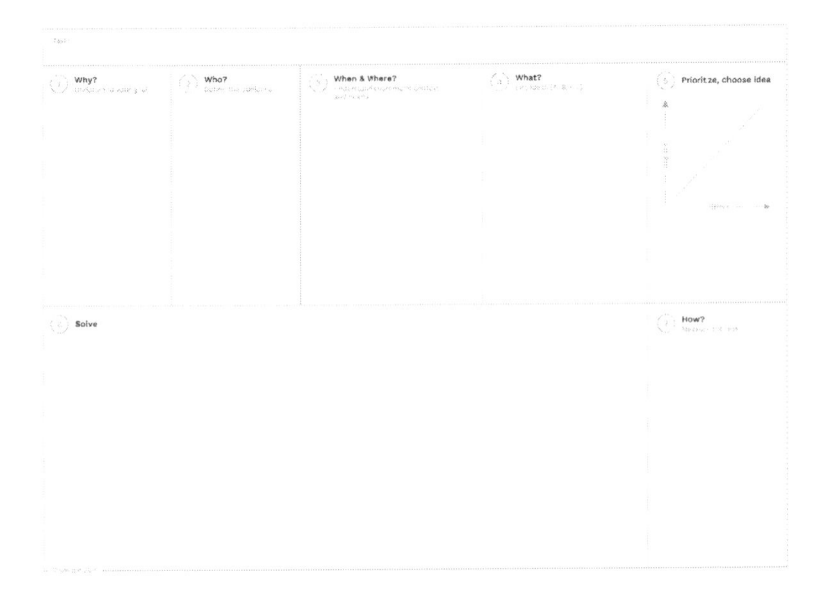

I prepared a framework canvas to guide you through the steps explained in chapter 2 and help you to remember the framework. You can print it on an A4 sheet of paper and practice solving the exercises at the end of this book. You can download the canvas at http://productdesigninterview.com/canvas.

Printed in Great Britain
by Amazon